A beat-up VW, filled with four young men, pulled up; the driver got out.

Sarah blocked his path, her outstretched hand shoving a ten dollar bill in his face.

"Would you guys buy me a fifth of vodka?" she asked.

"I don't think so."

"I'll do anything you want," she said, surprised by her own voice. "Anything . . ."

SARAH T.—
Portrait of a Teen-age Alcoholic

by Robin S. Wagner

Based on the
Universal Television Production
Written by RICHARD
and ESTHER SHAPIRO

BALLANTINE BOOKS • NEW YORK

Copyright © 1975 by Universal Studios, Inc.

All rights reserved under International and Pan-American Copyright Conventions. Published in the United States of America by Ballantine Books, a division of Random House, Inc., New York, and simultaneously in Canada by Random House of Canada Limited, Toronto.

ISBN 0-345-34242-9

Printed in Canada

First Edition: March 1975
Twenty-sixth Printing: December 1993

First Special Printing: March 1975
Second Special Printing: May 1975

Cover photograph by Bob Walker, using part of an NBC-TV photograph, originally appeared in *Scholastic Scope* magazine. Used by permission.

SARAH T.—
Portrait of a
Teen-age Alcoholic

Chapter One

Sarah tipped the glass up to her lips, hoping for one last drop. She was just starting to feel good and relaxed. It had been a hard week, the first in a new town, and the kids at this school seemed much more snobbish and clique-ish than at her old school. Why did I ever have to leave? Sara thought. Why did she ever have to marry *him*?

Damn, she thought, it's empty, and they were downstairs now. She could never get to the bar and feel the cool gin trickle down her parched throat. Why couldn't they have gone out tonight, as they had on every other night, so that she could sneak down and pour herself one more drink? That's all she needed, just one more drink before the guests started to arrive.

Tonight was a big event at the Hodges's home—the celebration of Matt's promotion to vice-president. Sarah didn't know that her stepfather was vice-president of, and she didn't care. All she knew was that her mother had run out and bought a new dress and had spent all day in the beauty shop getting her hair done.

She remembered the day of her mother's marriage to Matt Hodges, two years earlier. She had been thirteen and her sister Nancy, twenty, and just engaged herself.

"It's not every girl that gets to go to her own mother's wedding," her Aunt Martha had joked, cheeks flushed both with excitement and from the contents of the glass that she gripped tightly in her hand. "I bet this is really a treat for you, isn't it?"

"I'm having a wonderful time," Sarah had told her, hoping that all the well-wishers would disappear.

It was at Jean and Matt's wedding reception that Sarah had had her first taste of liquor. Nancy was off in a corner with her fiancé, and the newlyweds had no time for the skinny, brown-haired girl in the pink party dress. No one noticed the small, thin hand reaching for the cocktail from the serving tray. The drink had looked so appealing, and Sarah had noticed how the guests seemed to cheer up as soon as the amber liquid slid down their throats.

The drink, a whiskey sour, had a cherry floating on top and an orange slice arranged on the side of the glass. It looked almost too pretty to drink. Sarah ran into the ladies' room and took a sip. Sweet, but with a bitter aftertaste, it was a disappointment. She spat the first sip out in disgust. What is it that makes everyone so crazy about this stuff? she thought. It's awful. But, still, she took another sip, forcing herself to down it. If it makes all of them happy, it's got to have something to it. She made herself finish the entire cocktail, drinking it quickly in case anyone should want to use the bathroom. A slight buzzing sensation filled her ears, and her heavy, depressed mood suddenly lifted. She felt a little more sociable, more able to face the people outside. She opened the door slowly to make sure that no one was around. One of her mother's friends was coming down the hall in Sarah's direction. She didn't know what to do with the glass. She quickly rinsed it out in the sink and filled it with water.

"Hi, Sarah. How're ya doing?"

"Oh, hi, Mrs. Willis. It's so hot in there, I just

wanted a drink of water, and all the waiters were too busy."

"Wooonderful wedding, isn't it, dear," Mrs. Willis said. Sarah noticed that she had been drinking, too. "Your mother looks bootiful, just like a blushing bride."

"Yes, she does," Sarah said as she edged toward the door. She managed to get away and congratulated herself on her quick thinking.

That was how it had started, and now, two years later, it wasn't just an occasional drink that she needed. It was becoming a habit.

"Sarah, come on down," her mother called from the foot of the stairs. "The guests will be here any minute, and I need you to help Margaret serve."

"I'll be right down, Mom," Sarah called. She raised herself up from the bed and smoothed out her dress. Absently, she ran a comb through her long brown hair, looking at her plain face in the mirror. She wished she were beautiful like her mother or her sister Nancy. Maybe then she would make friends at school or get that boy, Ken Newkirk, to notice her.

Jean and Matt Hodges were proud of their new home, a $70,000 house set on a pleasantly wooded acre in Southern California. Matt, trim and in shape at forty-two, was a former military man. He carried himself as if he were still going into battle. And for him every day *was* a battle to get to the top. Tonight, in fact, was his victory celebration.

The living room in the Hodges's home was elegantly decorated, with an eye for the latest style. The long sectional sofa was covered in lush brown velvet. A low glass coffee table was positioned on a beautiful Oriental rug. Jean Hodges, tall, slender, with shoulder-length blond hair, was placing cocktail napkins on the coffee table when Sarah came down the stairs.

"Sarah, I wish you would do something with your

hair. Why does it have to look like you just got up?
There's going to be a lot of important people here, and
I want you to make a good impression."

"Oh, Mom, there's nothing wrong with my hair."

"Nothing that a good brushing wouldn't help. Now
go into the kitchen and help Margaret get the hors
d'oeuvres."

The door bell rang. Sarah could see her mother's
face tighten and her hand go to her own hair to give
it an extra pat before greeting her guests.

"Hurry up now, Sarah. They're starting to arrive.
And for God's sake, do something with your hair!"

"And how do you like your new school, Sarah?" a
strange woman asked her as she threaded her way
between the bodies. She had been serving drinks, but
the guests had also seen fit to put dirty dishes and
crumpled napkins on her tray.

Sarah looked up, surprised at being noticed.

"It's . . . fine . . ." she answered the strange woman.
What does she want to know about *me* for? Sarah
thought. All these strange faces and all these probing
questions. She felt as if she were on display, a monkey
dancing on a chain for the enjoyment of her mother's
and Matt's friends. Depositing the dirty glasses and
plates in the kitchen, she walked out into the living
room, where her mother was standing with a group of
admirers, as always. Wherever Jean went, she seemed
to have a following. She was the perfect hostess, always
putting everyone at ease at her parties. With her animated gestures and lively conversation, she was the
center of attention at any gathering. This evening, how-
ever, the people surrounding her were admiring
Nancy's new baby, Laurie.

"She's absolutely gorgeous, Jean," one woman was telling her.

"I swear, she looks like you," another piped up.

"How do you feel about being a grandmother?" the first one asked.

"Fine, since Liz Taylor made it fashionable."

They all laughed, the ice tinkling in their glasses. The baby started to cry.

"A lick of this'll quiet her down," a man suggested, sticking his finger in his glass and holding it out toward the baby's mouth. Sarah saw the look of discomfort in her mother's eyes.

"She must be wet, Mom. I'll change her," Sarah offered.

"Sure you want to?" her mother asked.

"Of course, she's my niece." And she took the squirming bundle from her mother's arms.

Show's over, little Laurie, Sarah mused. At least you're better at it than I am. Nobody thinks *I'm* cute, and they certainly won't offer *me* a lick of their drink.

Sarah went up to her room and laid the baby on the bed. Affectionately she said, "I bet you're about as glad as I am to be out of there . . . Do they ask you all the same kind of dumb questions they ask me? How do you like your new school? Dating a lot of boys? What clubs are you going to join? How would they like it if I asked them if they were having any good affairs . . ."

The baby cooed and poked her fingers in Sarah's mouth as if to agree with her assessment. Sarah held her close and thought she'd never ask Laurie if she liked her new school. She rocked Laurie in her arms, humming softly.

"Sarah!" Jean interrupted her thoughts. "Matt wants you to meet Mr. Peterson."

"What am I supposed to do with Laurie?"

"I'll put her to sleep. You try to make a good impression. You know how important this is to Matt."

Sarah went downstairs, picked up another tray, and walked into the living room. Mr. Peterson was Matt's new boss and Sarah knew that this entire party was to show him what a good choice he had made for his vice-president.

She approached the two men, who were deep in conversation. In contrast to Matt's well-preserved youth and leanness, Peterson was older and paunchier, but he had success and money written all over his face. They looked up at Sarah's approach.

"Oh, Sarah . . . you haven't met Mr. Peterson before. His son goes to your high school, you know."

Sarah knew all about Ray Peterson, better than they thought. He was one of Ken Newkirk's crowd and in the most popular group at school. Fat chance he would ever want to meet me, she thought, and shook her head in the negative.

"Well, you will. But you got to watch out for my son Ray. I know I'm his father, but I still feel it's my duty to warn you . . . he . . . *you* know." He gave her a sly wink. "Comes on a little with the girls. But a nice kid, you know what I mean? Doesn't smoke dope . . . doesn't pop pills . . ."

Peterson was obviously enjoying himself, expounding on the virtues of his son, and Sarah could see that he had put away a few drinks himself. She smiled demurely, hoping that she was making the "right" impression. Matt seemed distracted, as if he weren't too sure of himself. Sarah was surprised to see him so agitated; usually he was the epitome of self-confidence.

The door bell rang, and Matt jumped to get it. As he turned to the door, Sarah tapped him on the shoulder and motioned toward his drink.

"You done with that?" she asked hopefully. More

than ever, she craved the security of that drink now. She had the feeling that she couldn't handle one more person asking her about school, or boyfriends, or clubs. Matt finished off the drink, much to Sarah's dismay, and put it on her tray.

"What do you say, Sarah?" Mr. Peterson went on. "Shall I give Ray your phone number?"

"I'll tell you the truth, Mr. Peterson. I don't like blind dates, and I'm sure that Ray doesn't either."

Peterson looked disappointed. "At least let me buy you another drink," he said with a smile, as he put his empty glass on the tray Sarah was holding. Now, he was making sense, Sarah thought. Just get me a drink and *I'll* even call Ray.

"How about it?" Peterson repeated. "You gonna let me buy a drink?"

"I'm not allowed," Sarah responded, the picture of innocence.

Jean walked by, a self-satisfied smile on her face saying that her party was going along as planned.

"How about it, Jean? Kid's gotta learn to hold her liquor someday."

Sarah looked at her mother, who had hesitated at Peterson's question. Jean didn't want to offend her husband's boss, but she thought that a firm stand against allowing Sarah to drink was the best posture to take.

"Come on," Peterson urged. "I've just made Matt a v.p. and you're not gonna let this young lady drink to that?"

"She can have anything she wants—as long as it's ginger ale," Jean answered.

Peterson nodded for Sarah to follow him to the bar.

"Ginger ale it is," he said, as he filled two glasses with ice. Sarah sat on the bar stool, watching him pour the bourbon into one glass and the ginger ale into another.

He handed her the ginger ale, and then brought the bourbon to his lips.

"One rule I always tell my boy. If you drink, don't park—accidents make people." He laughed at his own joke. Sarah greedily watched as he gulped his drink.

It wasn't fair. These adults were having four and five and even six drinks, and all she wanted was one little drink to calm her nerves. She had enough to cope with—a new father, a new town, a new school, and *not one single friend*.

"Hey, Bob," Peterson called across the room. "One word before you go. Excuse me, young lady."

He moved to the door and left his glass sitting on the bar. It's too good to be true, Sarah thought as she stole her way into the kitchen, the half-filled glass clutched in her hand.

Margaret, the Hodges's maid, was washing dishes as Sarah entered.

"Margaret," Sarah lied, "Mom says we need more hors d'oeuvres in the living room."

Margaret had been with the Hodges since Jean had remarried, and she looked on Sarah with affection. Often she was the only one around for Sarah to confide in.

"Sure, hon," Margaret said as she picked up the tray. "What about you? You haven't eaten a thing all night. You all right?" she asked with concern.

"I'm all right, I guess. I bet you hate nights like this," Sarah said, as she and Margaret each took an hors d'oeuvre.

"Like what?"

"Like these parties. Having to wait on all those people."

"It's not so bad. I mean it's not one of my favorite

ways to spend an evening, but that's what I'm paid for."

Sarah smiled fondly as Margaret left the kitchen. Glancing around quickly to make sure she was alone, she raised the coveted glass to her lips and drank the bourbon as if her life depended on it. As she swallowed the last drop, a peculiar calm overtook her and she smiled benignly.

"At last," she murmured and went out to join the party.

Chapter Two

Jean opened the living room curtains. The morning's light flooded the disarray of the previous evening. Her head felt as if it were stuffed with cotton, and she shielded her eyes against the glare. She surveyed the scene of the battle. Her coffee table was covered with dirty glasses of every description. The hors d'oeuvres looked as if they had permanently merged with the plates. A chair was overturned in the corner. As she bent to pick it up, she noticed that one of her guests had spilled a drink on her rug. Jean made a mental note to mention it to Margaret when she arrived.

Sarah and Matt were silently finishing breakfast when Jean walked into the kitchen. Matt was at the stove, mixing a cup of instant coffee. Sarah slumped over a bowl of cold cereal, her expression one of discomfort.

"Thank goodness Margaret's coming back this morning. If I had to face this mess alone, I'd throw myself under a truck. Sarah, is that all you're eating for breakfast? I tell you, Matt," she said with pride, "that must have been some terrific party, because I've got a hangover you wouldn't believe."

"Here, try this for your hangover," Matt said to Jean as he handed her a cup of coffee. She accepted it gratefully, and he began to massage the back of her neck.

As she sipped the coffee, she said to Sarah, "Isn't today the day you try out for the glee club?"

Sarah looked up from her breakfast glumly and nodded her head. She wasn't feeling too well from last night either, but she didn't want her mother to know.

"Pick out what you're going to sing?"

"I haven't decided yet."

At her mother's urging, Sarah had decided to try out for the glee club. She was going to sing a Bob Dylan song which she knew probably wouldn't go over with the glee club girls. But Sarah loved blues and rock music and played deep, thoughtful tunes on her guitar. Since she loved to sing, she thought she would give it a chance.

Jean's attention was now focused on re-living the events of the previous night.

"Did you see your boss—did you see old million-dollar Peterson trying to make it out to his silver-gray limousine?"

"I thought he'd never go home," Matt laughed with his wife.

"Go home? I thought he was going to spend the night on our front lawn."

Sarah watched her parents with a cynical expression. They were just like kids, boasting of their drinking prowess, trying to top the other.

"Well," Matt said, trying for one-upmanship, "what about your fancy friend, Mrs. . . . you know who I mean, the blond with the short husband . . ."

"What about her?"

"Very classy lady, right?" He stood up, pantomiming the blond, " 'Excuse me, Matt, but I'm going to step out for a bit of air.' Then she breaks the Olympic

record for the thirty-seven-yard dash—down the driveway and into the rose garden and then, ugh . . ."

Jean doubled over with laughter at the thought of
her friend. "That's disgusting," she said at Matt's
imitation. "You're making it up."

"Am I?" Matt asked, enjoying her reaction. "That
woman holds her liquor like a broken glass."

Sarah was nervous enough about trying out for the
glee club. But what upset her more was that her
mother didn't seem to notice. All she could do was
laugh at the dumb antics of her friends, Sarah thought
as she collected her books.

Jean was oblivious to her daughter's movements.

"Too bad she doesn't have your wooden leg," she
teased Matt.

"Complaining?" he asked with a wink.

"Nope. Impressed. I've never seen a man drink so
much and still be able to do . . ." she looked at Sarah,
"do forty push-ups . . . before bed."

Matt gave her a knowing look that did not escape
Sarah.

"Want to know my secret, Sarah?" Matt asked her.
"Little trick I picked up in the Philippines . . ."

"I know." She had heard the story many times
before, especially after one of Matt's "celebrations."
"You always take a tablespoon of cocoa butter before
you drink," she mimicked.

"Oh, well, then, here's one I never told you . . .
always have at least one drink with a twist. That way
you'll never get scurvy." Matt and Jean broke up with
laughter.

"Aren't you going to finish your breakfast?" Jean
asked, suddenly attentive to Sarah's needs.

"I gotta leave. I'm not very hungry anyway . . ."

"What was the name of the club Elaine's mother

was talking about last night?" Jean asked with interest.

Sarah was anxious to get out of the house.

"The Junior Antisex League," she answered curtly.

"You don't have to be snitty about it."

"Mom, I'm doing just fine in this school," she said with exasperation. "I'm already making plenty of friends. So why don't you just stop worrying about me?"

"Hey, you want me to drive you to school?" Matt asked.

"No thanks."

Sarah walked out the door to the shed where she kept her bicycle. Her parents seemed only to care what clubs she joined and who her friends were; they didn't care what was going on inside of her, the fear that she had about not making friends, and the difficulty she had adjusting to a new school and new teachers.

Jean looked after Sarah for a second and then gave Matt a puzzled look. But as soon as her daughter was out of her line of vision, she continued:

"God, what a nine-carat, brass-plated headache. Must have been some fantastic party . . ."

Sarah pushed the red ten-speed bicycle that Matt had given her the first day of school down the driveway. She really loved the ride to school, but the first day she pedaled up, the kids had given her curious stares. It was certainly different in her old neighborhood, where everyone rode their bikes to school. Matt was much more successful than Sarah's father, and he had moved his new wife and daughter to a much more prosperous neighborhood. The kids never rode bicycles to school, but arrived in shiny new sports cars or on motorcycles. Sarah had earned the reputation of an oddball the very first day. She wore her new wealth awkwardly, and she wasn't as glib about her parents' resources as some of her classmates.

As Sarah prepared to mount her bike, a metallic-blue Camaro screeched to a halt across the street. The driver honked the horn impatiently. Sarah recognized Ken Newkirk as the driver. What a creep she looked like, Sarah thought, wanting to disappear, with her red bicycle and book bag slung over her shoulder.

Marsha Cooper appeared at the front door and gave Ken a wave. She came bounding out of the house, her blond hair flying behind her, her miniskirt and skimpy sweater doing justice to her figure.

She stood with her hands on her hips until the boy seated next to Ken got out and let her sit next to her boyfriend. She snuggled up to Ken and pecked him on the cheek.

Sarah was too preoccupied with the scene in the car to notice Margaret walking up the sidewalk. But Margaret had watched the car drive away and had seen Sarah looking after it longingly.

"You'll do just fine, love, you'll see," she told Sarah. Getting on her bike, Sarah looked over her shoulder and smiled meekly at Margaret. She rode off in the direction of the car.

The high school Sarah attended was set on an expansive lawn and landscaped with trees and shrubs. Three tennis courts, an outdoor basketball court, and two football fields surrounded the one-story building. A circular drive led to the front door. In the lobby, Sarah read on the activities board that the glee club would meet at noon.

The morning went by quickly for Sarah. She had

English, art and then math. During the last half of her math class she started to feel anxious about the tryouts. So much depended on her being chosen. Maybe then her mother would stop pestering her about fitting in. Sarah wished that she had a little drink to tide her over now, just until she was finished with the tryouts. This was going to be the hardest situation she'd had to cope with since her parents' divorce. Torn between being herself and being the person her mother wanted her to be, Sarah felt confused and alone.

The third-period bell sounded, and the stirring students brought Sarah back to reality and the matter at hand. With a nod of determination, she strode down the hall.

As she entered the dark, quiet auditorium, she noticed a lone girl, illuminated on the bare stage, already singing. When the girl on stage finished her song, the tight group of club members in the audience conferred. The president of the glee club emerged with the verdict.

"That's fine, Judy," she pronounced magnanimously. "Glee club meets here Tuesday and Thursday at noon." And then she turned to face the nearly empty auditorium. "Sarah Travis is next."

At the sound of her name, Sarah froze in her seat. She was gripped by almost uncontrollable anxiety. She wanted to run, to escape and disappear. She could feel the eyes of the other applicants on her.

"Sarah Travis . . ." the president said with annoyance. "Is she here?"

Trying to collect her thoughts, Sarah shuffled through the papers in her notebook, looking for her music. She managed to find it, even with her shaking hands, and started out of the row, stepping on toes and dropping papers as she pushed her way through.

"If you're not ready, Sarah, we'll come back to you," the president went on, sensing Sarah's discomfort.

"I'm ready," she said, as she moved toward the girl playing the piano and handed her the sheet music. Out of the corner of her eye, she noticed that Marsha Cooper was trying out also.

On the stage, Sarah felt exposed, an insect on a pin. She looked at the girls clustered together, whispering and giggling, Sarah felt, at her. They stared up at her like buzzards on a rail. The pianist started the first few bars of Sarah's song. She cleared her throat, but the words wouldn't come out.

"Could you . . . could you start again, please?" Sarah asked, embarrassed and flustered.

The girl at the piano glanced at the president who nodded her head with authority. The music started again, and Sarah sang the first few lines with emphasis. As she began the chorus, she realized that she couldn't go on. She searched for the next line, but her mind was blank. Recovering, she picked it up, but hit a wrong note. Its sharpness rang out in the silent auditorium. The pianist stopped, her hands poised on the keys. Every eye in the auditorium was focused on Sarah now. Gathering her courage, she was about to ask for another chance, when the president cut her off:

"Thank you for trying out, Sarah," she said coldly. "Harriet Bernstein is next . . ."

"I think if I could just try it once more . . ."

"You do that. You come back and see us next semester . . . Harriet . . . ?" she went on; Sarah was already a memory.

Sarah felt the tears welling up in her eyes. Head bowed, she left the stage, walking past the gauntlet of upturned, slightly superior faces, as Harriet began the first bars of her song.

She walked through the empty hall, wandering listlessly. She felt foolish and humiliated. The bell rang, but she didn't seem to notice. She merged with the stream of students filling up the hall. All around her, kids were laughing, shoving and joking, but Sarah was alone in her thoughts. As Sarah walked down the hall, she was shoved from behind. Her thoughts were rudely interrupted, and her books went flying.

"I'm sorry. Guess I wasn't looking. Here, let me get those for you."

Sarah looked up into the friendly, smiling face of Ken Newkirk. Tall, blond, with soft brown eyes, he was very appealing. He bent to retrieve her books.

"Haven't I seen you?" he asked, handing them to her. "Don't you live across the street from Marsha Cooper?"

"Uh huh . . ."

"You ride your bike to school?"

"Well . . . sometimes," Sarah said with embarrassment.

He piled the last book on her arm.

"By the way, I'm Ken Newkirk."

"Sarah Travis."

"Well, sorry about the books. I'll see you around."

Dumbfounded, Sarah remained in the hall, watching him walk away. Then, rearranging her books, she shrugged her shoulders and entered the stream of students. Her next class was science and she wasn't doing well in it at all. Walking slowly, she was jostled by the rushing latecomers. The bell rang, signaling the start of the next period. Sarah stood outside her classroom, watching the door slam in her face. She just couldn't go in. Suddenly, she was gripped by a longing to see the familiar face of her father. She missed him terribly and ached to hear his voice. Heading across the campus, she searched for a phone booth.

Jerry Travis had often said, "I don't care if I never

get rich." Watching him put the fininishing touches on a portrait or a landscape, Sarah felt that the moments she and her father spent in his studio were the best she had ever had. Only then did she feel loved and needed.

Jerry Travis had always wanted to make his living from his art, but Jean had wanted him to take a steadier job. Forced to take a position as a salesman for an art supply house, he hated it; the traveling, the long hours, the hustling he had to do to stay on top.

Jerry had tried to fill Jean's expectations by taking the job. The house was calm and peaceful while he was away on business trips. Jean was cheerful, a different person. But Sarah, even at a young age, knew that there was something wrong with her parents' marriage.

"If it weren't for the children, I'd leave you right now," Sarah would often hear her mother scream. Feeling left out and hurt, Sarah would run to her room and cry.

"We'll just go off, the two of us, I promise," Jerry had told her as he packed his bags and left the house for good. "Maybe to Oregon . . ."

"I'll miss you, honey. But anytime you need me, just give me a call."

She needed him now, she thought, looking through her purse for some change to make the call. She dialed the operator.

"I'd like to make a long distance call to San Francisco."

Dropping the required change into the phone, Sarah held her breath and waited for her father to answer. The phone rang twice, three times, four times. Sarah held it to her ear and counted twenty rings. He wasn't there. She needed him now and he wasn't there. Sitting in the booth, she fought back the tears.

". . . Well, if he's not in his room, would you please try paging him in the restaurant? I'll hold."

Sarah looked up from the phone. She sensed someone was in the room. Jean, who had been standing in the shadows, stepped forward.

"I know it's a long distance call. But you can take it out of my allowance," she said defensively.

"Sarah, you know that's not necessary. You can call your father any time you want." Jean's voice was gentle, and she was genuinely concerned. "But you can't expect him to come all the way back from San Francisco just because . . ."

"He'll come."

"Even if he does—then what?"

"Maybe he can fix it so I can go back to the old school."

"Why would you want to go back to the old school anyway? You weren't so happy there . . ."

Sarah heard the operator's voice on the other end.

"Would you try the lobby once more, then? *Please,* it's very important."

Jean was troubled at this lack of communication with her daughter. She felt frustrated at being shut out of Sarah's life, as if a wall had been built between them.

Sarah listened intently for her father's voice.

"Sarah . . . listen . . . maybe if you tried to discuss it with Matt . . ."

"I don't want to talk to Matt. I want to talk to my father."

The realization of the distance between her and Sarah brought tears to Jean's eyes.

"Why do you treat Matt as if he doesn't exist? He tries to be nice to you. He's trying to make a life for us."

A relieved smile overcame Sarah's serious face.

"Yes, operator," she said expectantly, "I'm still holding."

But Jean was unable to contain her anger. "Don't you think it would be easier for Matt if you *did* go to live with your father? Do you suppose he needs to support another man's family?"

Sarah, her hand clamped tightly over the mouth-piece, glared fiercely at her mother. Realizing the cruelty of her remark, Jean went on, "I'm sorry, that was a bit . . . out of line. But . . ."

Sarah hadn't heard her last words. Her face bright-ened, and her tears started to brim over.

"Daddy . . . it's me, Sarah . . . Just a minute."

She looked up at Jean, waiting for her to leave. Jean looked sadly at her daughter and turned to go. Solemnly, she walked into the living room just as Matt was entering the front door.

"What kind of a face is that to greet a vice-president?" he asked. "Is something wrong?"

"Not really . . ." she told him, trying to cover up her unhappiness.

In the den, Sarah could be heard saying good-bye to her father.

As she entered the living room, Matt asked her, "You two been sniping at each other again?"

Tranquillity had replaced Sarah's troubled expres-sion. Jean, too, had softened.

"Sarah . . . honey . . . I hate to see you set yourself up for a disappointment."

"I know, Mom," Sarah said quietly. "But you were wrong. Because . . . you see . . . he's coming. Day after tomorrow." She smiled broadly. "My daddy's coming."

Chapter Three

Feathery clouds floated across an azure sky. Crashing pale green waves pounded against the rocks of the Palos Verdes. A renewed Sarah, full of laughter and joy, was seated on a boulder, gazing at her father with adoring eyes.

"I guess things just aren't gonna be as bad as I thought they'd be."

"The way you sounded on the phone, all I expected to find was a little puddle of salty tears," Jerry Travis said as he bit into a tuna sandwich that Sarah had prepared for their picnic. Lounging on the rocks, enjoying each other's company and their lunch, Sarah and Jerry looked more like friends than father and daughter. He had the kind of face that never seemed to age, and his smile was eternally youthful. Beaming, Sarah plied him with hard-boiled eggs, potato salad, and her own home-baked apple pie.

"Daddy?" Sarah, suddenly serious, asked. "Are you mad at me? I mean for dragging you all the way down here for nothing?"

"You're not nothing, Sarah," Jerry answered thoughtfully. "You're the most important thing in this whole bloodshot world to me—you and your sister."

"But I wouldn't want to mess up your job or anything."

"I don't want to talk about jobs," he said firmly. "I want to hear about the boy."

Blushing, Sarah became animated. "Well, his name's Kenny Newkirk, and he called me up and invited me to go to this party at Ray Peterson's house . . ." she said with pride.

They walked down the beach, hand in hand. Pants rolled to the knees, they splashed through the waves.

". . . and he's a junior, which means he's almost seventeen. I don't think that's too old for me, do you? And he's only gorgeous. And he has his own horse, too, that he may let me ride sometime." Her enthusiastic gestures emphasized each point.

Jerry was contemplative; he didn't want his little girl to be letting herself in for a disappointment, but Sarah's apparent happiness couldn't be ignored.

She mistook her father's expression for disapproval. "What's the matter?"

"My little girl's gone and fallen in love with one gorgeous seventeen-year-old cowboy and I'm just mildly insane with jealousy, that's all," he kidded her.

Picking up on her father's teasing, Sarah put her arms around him and said coyly, "Daddy, I hardly know him. You know that's the truth," she said, almost to herself. "The only time he ever spoke to me was once when he knocked me down in the hall."

"Obviously he wanted to meet you. You're lucky he didn't run you over with his horse."

Oblivious to her father's comments, Sarah went on, "I mean, it's not as if I was the prettiest girl in the school or anything."

The yellow Frisbee sailed through the air. As Sarah ran to retrieve it, Jerry tackled her from behind. Sand flew in their eyes, their hair. Sarah's face was almost buried as she lay on top of the Frisbee. Jerry tickled her until she yielded. He grabbed it away from her and held it over his head, in mock defiance of her pleas. Finally, he surrendered the Frisbee to her.

"Say, kid, what are you doing away from school on a weekday anyhow? You're not cutting, are you?"

Sarah was silent. Turning to face him, she asked, "What are you doing away from your job? You still have one, don't you?" Her voice was suddenly strained.

Jerry hung his head as if he were a delinquent child. He threw the Frisbee over Sarah's head.

"You missed it. Let's go," he said, as he ran toward it.

"Daddy . . ." Sarah continued. "You do *still* have a job?"

"Well, not exactly."

"Oh, Daddy," she said, her hands on her hips.

"Just grab me another beer, there, puss, before you start sounding like your mother." He tousled her hair affectionately and picked up the Frisbee. Sarah followed him, the six-pack in her hand. Jerry finished one can, crushing it and tossing it into the ocean.

"That doesn't impress me. And besides, you're polluting the ocean."

"Sorry, babe, hand me another one." He popped the top off and took a long draw. Sarah watched him suspiciously. By his third can, Jerry was staggering across the beach, Sarah dragging behind with the half-empty six-pack.

He smiled at her, boyishly. ". . . So there I was, walking across the Gabriel River Bridge." He demonstrated his brisk, well-mannered walk. "And I stopped dead, in the middle . . . and I said to myself, 'Jerry, what the hell am I doing with my life?' Dragging my aspirations up and down the state, sweating to meet sales quotas, selling art supplies for *other* people to use, getting so fed up sometimes I'd like to" —he stumbled on a large shell and lost his balance.

Leaning on Sarah, he continued. "I've got some talent,
I really do," he said, almost too convincingly. "More
than a lot of these punks just out of art school who
are getting one-man shows in every gallery and barn
and outhouse that has an empty wall. Is it my fault
I had responsibilities, and I had to go out and take
a square job?" He looked at Sarah guiltily. "Not that
I'm blaming your mother, mind you." And then a
blank look came over his face and he continued,
"Anyway, there I was, standing in the middle of that
bridge, and I said to myself, 'What would happen—I
mean, what would be the world-shattering consequences—if I were just to toss this sample case out
into the river' "—he drew back the arm holding
the beer can—" 'as far as I' "—winding it up, he
tossed it into the ocean—" 'can?' "

"You didn't," Sarah replied, a laugh rising in her
throat. He could make her so happy, sharing his jokes
and his memories of their past life together. His
presence warmed her like the sun, and she wished
they could go on like this forever.

"What are you going to do now?" she asked, after
they had ambled for a while.

"You know what I'd like to do?"

"Go to Oregon." It was their dream.

"It's a perfect time."

"For the both of us," Sarah said, tears forming at
the corners of her eyes. "I'd love it."

Jerry picked up on the fantasy.

"Just a little place off in the woods somewhere. Lay
in a bunch of canvases and some decent oils."

"And all you'd have to do is paint all day and not
worry about sales quotas and delivery dates."

"Sounds awful good, doesn't it, puss?"

"Let's do it, Daddy," Sarah said exuberantly. "Let's
just take off and do it."

Jerry looked into the shining, cheerful face of his daughter. He adored her and wanted only the best for her. Realizing that he couldn't provide it, he gently returned them to reality.

"But what would we eat?" he asked halfheartedly. "Pictures of pastrami sandwiches?"

"We'll get along, Daddy. I'll get a job after school . . ."

But the balloon had already burst for Jerry, and he said candidly, "And what about your mother? She thinks I'm some kind of a corrupting influence."

It was all right for him to dream; he had faced the letdown many times and emerged only faintly scarred. But he wanted something more for his daughter.

"Do you suppose for a minute she'd give up custody?" He looked directly into Sarah's eyes. She avoided his. "Well, would she?"

"I guess not."

He hadn't meant to be so harsh, but she was becoming too dependent on him. She sat silently, the waves lapping at her feet, thin arms wrapped protectively around her knees. They both stared out at the ocean. Finally, Jerry broke the trance.

"We'll do it, puss."

"When?"

He started to get up, brushing the sand from his pants. He held out his hand, but she didn't take it. She stayed where she was.

"One day soon, I promise. But right now I want you to take this." He pulled his wallet from his pocket and took out a few bills. "Buy yourself a new dress or something."

"Daddy, this is fifty dollars. And you don't even have a job."

"Don't worry about it," Jerry said confidently. "I've already got something better lined up. With the third biggest art supply house in the state. And I want my Sarah to be the prettiest girl at the party."

"Daddy, I love you," she said as she stood up and kissed him on the cheek.

"I love you too, puss."

They started back toward the car. "And tell that cowboy, one step out of line and he'll have to shoot it out . . . with me."

"Race you to the car," Sarah shouted, their moment of seriousness forgotten.

"I'll give you a head start," Jerry said as he watched his carefree daughter run down the beach.

Chapter Four

Standing before her bedroom mirror, Sarah surveyed her new outfit. She had spent only half the money her father had given her, saving the rest for his next visit to do something special. But now, as she tucked the peach-colored sweater into the long blue-denim skirt, she felt pretty good, as if something special were about to happen to her. For the first time in many months, she was happy and liked herself. She hadn't felt the need for a drink since the day Kenny Newkirk had bumped into her in the hall in school. And the fact that he had asked her to Ray's party only added to her blossoming self-confidence.

Her long brown hair shone, and she gave it a few extra strokes with the hard-bristled brush. Looking at her pert profile in the mirror, she was pleased with the image. Even her skin had cleared up for the occasion.

Entering the living room, Sarah heard her mother and sister discussing Laurie's new clothes.

"I'm borrowing your scarf, Mom," Sarah said, as she tied a pale blue kerchief under her chin.

Her mother was too preoccupied with the baby to notice.

Sarah walked over to the car bed and smiled at Laurie, who squirmed and whimpered in recognition.

"Can I pick her up?" Sarah asked.

"Honey," Jean said, "you can't pick up a baby every time it whimpers. You'll spoil it."

"But I just want to hold her a minute."

"She's got to sleep now," Nancy broke in. "You can come by one afternoon and play with her if you like." She tucked a blanket around the baby, and glancing up at Sarah, noticed. "Hey, isn't that the outfit you bought with the money Daddy gave you?"

"Uh huh."

"Cute," she said, as she turned her attention to her baby.

Sarah waited for her mother's approval, but Jean was too concerned with Nancy's purchases to respond. They held up each tiny piece of clothing, admiring the detail and the craftsmanship.

Sarah walked to the hall mirror to check herself out once more.

"Who are you going out with tonight?" Nancy asked.

"Just a boy."

"Not *just* a boy at all," Jean spoke up, at once attentive. "He just happens to be the vice-president of the junior class and captain of the swimming team." She reeled off his qualifications as if he were running for office.

"How'd you know that?" Sarah asked.

"I guess his mother may have mentioned it to me." She eyed her mother suspiciously.

"Is that how you got fixed up with him?" Nancy wondered.

Sarah's mouth dropped. She studied Jean carefully. "I didn't know you knew his mother."

"I met her a couple of times."

Becoming more enraged, Sarah said, "You never told *me* that."

"Didn't I?"

"Mom, did you say anything to her about Ken taking me out or anything like that?"

"No. Why would I do that?" Jean, noticeably flustered, tried to cover up. "I mean . . . I did mention that . . . we had kids about the same age . . . and wouldn't it be nice if . . . some time. . . ."

"I knew," Sarah screamed, shaken and hurt by her mother's insensitive meddling. "I knew he wouldn't be interested in me." How could she face him, now that she knew he was only doing it at the urging of his mother. The humiliation was too much for her to bear, and she crumbled onto the couch in tears.

"Sarah, stop it," Jean said sternly.

"How could you do a thing like this to me?" she wailed.

"I was only trying to help. We're new in the neighborhood, and you don't know many of the kids, and the situation just sort of came up."

Sarah had herself under control now and faced her mother with fury.

"You mean *you* made it come up!"

"I've never stopped you from making friends on your own, Sarah. I did this for you. Can't you appreciate that?"

"I'm not going," Sarah stated flatly. "I'm not." Stamping her foot, she took off her mother's scarf and threw it to the floor.

"I'm going to lock myself in my room, and when he gets here, you can tell him."

She stormed toward the stairs that led to her room. The door bell rang. They all stood frozen in their places, as if they were a frame in a movie film.

Jean returned to action first. "Tell him what?"

Sarah refused to answer her mother. She just stood by the banister, gripping it until her hand turned white.

"I went to a lot of trouble to arrange this, Sarah,"

Jean continued, her voice hard. "If you embarrass me . . ."

Letting the threat hang, Jean walked toward the door and opened it, wearing her impeccable hostess-face.

A nervous, well-groomed Ken stood before them, dressed in a light blue button-down shirt and pressed Levis.

"Is Sarah ready?" he asked with a tense smile.

"Why, you must be Ken," Jean said.

"Yes, ma'am."

"Sarah," Jean called as if nothing had happened, "Ken's here."

Nancy, who had been sitting, wide-eyed and quiet, during the whole argument, moved toward Sarah. "Go on," she urged her sister, giving her a gentle pat on the back.

Sarah stepped forward, as if she were approaching a firing squad. She wiped her eyes and smoothed her hair and put on her coat.

"Hi."

"Hi. Well, I guess we better get going. Nice meeting you, Mrs. Hodges."

"Bye now, and have a good time," Jean called after them as they left the house.

When they reached Ken's car, he mechanically opened the door for Sarah, but she hesitated before getting in.

"I'm sorry you got roped into this," she blurted out.

"Forget it," he said coldly.

"If you want, you could just drop me at a movie."

"Hey, it's okay," Ken said, a little annoyed. "C'mon . . . we'll have fun anyway." He gave her an encouraging smile.

They drove in silence to Ray Peterson's house, which was on the other side of town. Sarah stole a look at

Ken, who was staring directly ahead as he drove. She loved the way he looked: wavy blond hair reaching to his collar, a straight nose with a sprinkling of freckles. He had such a kind face, she thought, maybe tonight won't be so bad after all.

They arrived at the Petersons' house, which was all aglow. Cars were lined up in the driveway, spilling into the street. Ken had to park a few houses down. Walking up to the front door, they could hear the music blaring. No one answered the door bell, so Ken tried the front door; it was open. He walked in, Sarah lagging behind, trying to work up her courage to face a houseful of strangers.

At Ken's entrance, it seemed to Sarah that the whole room of people ran over to greet him. He didn't introduce her, and the others just ignored her as if she were invisible. Taking off her coat, she sat down on the nearest chair and remained conspicuously alone.

Marsha Cooper made her way over to Ken. "How's the mercy date going?"

"Okay." He shrugged his shoulders.

"Want to dance with me?"

He sighed. "Yeah, I do. But it wouldn't be fair to her."

"Oh yeah, right," Marsha teased. "Never interfere with a social worker in the pursuit of his duty."

She gave his arm a loving squeeze and went to join a group around the thin, curly-haired guitar player.

Ken started to move toward Sarah, who looked so pathetically isolated, but Ray distracted him. He pantomimed a drink, and Ken followed him out of the room.

Observing Ken and Marsha in conversation, Sarah figured that they had been discussing her. She had also noticed Ken and Ray going out of the room and wished that she had followed her first instincts and locked

herself in her bedroom for the night. Yet she had
wanted so badly to have fun tonight, to fit in with the
kids, to make her mother proud of her.

"Weren't you at the glee club tryouts the other day?"
Marsha Cooper had sidled up to her. She was grinning
maliciously, from ear to ear.

"Yes," Sarah said glumly.

"Shame you didn't make it."

Sarah didn't have the patience for a showdown with
Marsha. It wasn't her fault that Ken had listened to his
mother and invited her along. She stood up, looking
around for Ken to tell him that she wanted to leave. It
was enough humiliation for one night.

"Looking for Ken?"

"No . . . no, I'm not. Excuse me."

She made her way through the crowd of bodies and
found her coat. It had been put on the bed in the guest
room. She slipped it on and started for the door.

"Sarah . . . where are you going?" Ken asked, entering the bedroom.

Looking at him solmenly, she replied, "I just thought
I'd go on home."

"How you gonna get there?"

"Take a bus or something."

"Don't be dumb, Sarah," he said, taking her hand.
"Come on in here."

She dropped her coat on the bed and then they
walked into Mr. Peterson's study. Ken closed the big,
oak double doors. Ray and a few other boys were busy
mixing drinks at the bar. Bottles of every kind of
liquor imaginable were lined up in rows. Ray, pouring
some gin into a glass, looked surprised at Sarah's being
there.

"Hey, Ken," he said with alarm, "what are you
doing?"

"Fix her one, too."

"Listen, if my old man gets on to this . . ."

"She's cool," Ken told him, "and besides, she's my date."

"Okay, okay, man."

Although she felt as if she really needed a drink now, Sarah thought it would be better if she declined, not wanting to seem too eager.

"I don't think I should."

"Come on," Ken urged her, "it won't hurt you. Just one—that's all we're gonna have."

"Well . . . maybe . . . just one."

Ray poured some gin into a glass. He filled it halfway and then, looking at Sarah, he smirked and filled it about three-quarters full.

"Take it easy," Ken said. "You want to get her zonked?"

Ray gave him a sly wink. Next to Ray, a boy poured just the right amount of water into the gin bottle to camouflage the loss. Ray poured some coke into Sarah's glass.

"And a little something to make the medicine go down," he said, enjoying his bartending. He handed Sarah the drink.

Sarah anxiously awaited the reassuring taste of the gin. Not wanting Ken to think she was too familiar with drinking, though, she crinkled her nose coquettishly.

"This stuff tastes awful."

"It takes a little getting used to," Ken told her with the air of an expert. He picked up his glass, and they moved toward the door.

"Come on, Sarah, let's go in and dance. I'll introduce you to some of the kids." He put his arm around her protectively.

Sarah took a sip of the drink and looked up at Ken thoughtfully. "Sure, Ken. I guess I'll stay a while longer."

The party had been going on for over an hour. Ken had properly introduced Sarah to a few of the kids, who had all politely acknowledged her and then returned to their private conversations. Sarah finished her drink quickly, but she didn't want to ask Ken for a refill. She had remembered her mother's warning that boys didn't like girls who drank: "It's just not feminine to walk around with a drink in your hand."

Sarah waited until Ken was involved in a conversation.

"Excuse me," she said as she moved toward the bathroom. Instead, she slipped into Mr. Peterson's study, closing the doors quietly behind her. She ran over to the bar, knocking over a glass in her haste. Behind the bar, she looked for the gin bottle. Taking a healthy swallow, she breathed deeply as the warm liquor deliciously burned her throat. Her eyes sparkled, and a smile of relief graced her face. She started to re-cap the bottle but then decided to take one more swallow. Licking her lips appreciatively, she put the bottle back on the shelf and turned to go out of the room.

Ken was seated on the couch in the living room. He looked up at Sarah's entrance. She looked different, but he couldn't put his finger on it; more at ease, more confident.

"I thought you athlete types weren't supposed to drink," she said, her shyness replaced by an easy-going sensuality.

"I don't much. Actually, I don't care for the taste either."

Marsha, who had observed Sarah's transformation, strode across the room and whispered into the ear of the guitar player, Jim. He nodded his head and began to play the song that Sarah had used for the glee club tryouts.

Sarah and Ken were too engrossed in their conversation to notice. Marsha, with an insidious smile, came up to them.

"Hey, Sarah Travis—he's playing your song."

"Did you arrange that for me?" Sarah asked, impervious to Marsha's threat. "How sweet."

"Why don't you join in. I'm sure he wouldn't mind."

Aware that she was being challenged, Sarah considered it for a moment. She was feeling good, really good, and she knew that if she got up there to sing, she would sing her heart out, the way she had wanted to at the tryouts. Returning Marsha's stare, she rose, picked up her glass, and drained the few drops still in it. Marsha took over Sarah's vacated place on the couch. She slipped her arm through Ken's and sat down, as if she were a Roman preparing to watch the lions devour a hapless gladiator.

Sarah moved into the center of the room, motioning to Jim to begin again. All the chatter in the room had stopped. A few kids brought their chairs closer to Sarah. She commanded all their attention. In a clear, lilting voice, she began. Faces around her were shining, bodies swaying with the music. Jim smiled warmly and harmonized in the background. Sarah's head was whirling, but she held it high, singing to the ceiling, the sky, her father. . .

Breathless, she finished, her heart pounding. Ken was the first to applaud, slipping free of Marsha's arm. Her brilliant plan to embarrass Sarah foiled, Marsha's face clouded. A few kids went up to Sarah, begging her to sing again, but she brushed them off.

"That was good, Sarah," Ken said to her with respect. "I mean, that was really good."

She started to walk away.

"You're not leaving, are you?"

"No," Sarah said, looking at Marsha boldly. "I think I'll stay for a while."

She walked into the bedroom, as if she wanted to get something from her coat pocket but on her way to join the others in the living room, she made a quick detour into the study.

She went for the gin bottle but put that down, not wanting to use up all the gin, and reached for the Scotch instead. Taking a few swallows, she replaced the cap and returned, energized, to the party. Tapping Ken on the shoulder, she pointed to the dance floor.

"You're really moving," he said to a bouncing Sarah, after they had danced a few numbers. "What'd Ray put in your drink," he joked, "pep pills?"

She just smiled.

Sarah felt as if she could go on all night, but after a while Ken wanted to sit down.

"Let's stop, Sarah, I'm tired."

"Okay, but I'm thirsty. Let's get a drink."

"I think you've had enough," he teased.

"No, I mean of water. I'm dying of thirst."

In the kitchen, a few boys and girls were clustered around a wineskin. Sarah walked to the kitchen sink and turned on the tap, all the while watching the wineskin being passed back and forth.

A tall, long-haired boy passed it to Ken. He squirted it into his mouth delicately and passed it on to Sarah. In her excitement, Sarah grabbed it greedily, held it to her mouth and missed, the ruby-colored liquid spilling down her new sweater. She didn't seem to mind, and she held the pouch up to her mouth again. This time she directed the stream accurately and drank liberally. Ken watched in amazement.

"Come on, let's get something to eat, I'm famished." He grabbed her hand and led her into the living room. He filled two plates and handed her one. She took it weakly, allowing some of the contents to fall to the floor. Ken gave her a quizzical look.

"You're not getting high, are you?" He looked concerned. "Maybe I shouldn't have given you anything to drink."

"I'm fine," Sarah mumbled, hardly able to keep her head up.

After a few minutes, Marsha approached them, and Ken said, "You want anything? I'm going to get seconds."

Sarah shook her head. She was feeling nauseous now and a little feeble.

"If you don't eat, how are you gonna grow up to be big and strong?" Marsha inquired, sticking out her chest. "Raquel Welch ate all her potato salad."

Standing up, weaving slightly, Sarah started to walk toward the bedroom to lie down.

But Marsha kept digging. "I mean, if you don't get all your vitamins, how are you gonna ride your bicycle?"

At that, Sarah, without warning, surprising even herself, picked up the full plate and heaved it all over Marsha's chest. And, literally adding insult to injury, she gave Marsha a shove that sent her crashing into a table next to the couch. The table tipped over. An expensive-looking glass and chrome lamp tumbled to the floor, broken pieces flying all over.

Marsha, speechless for once, glared at Sarah ferociously. Ken heard the noise and ran to Sarah's side.

"Oh boy, wait until my old man sees this." Ray was pulling Marsha out of the tangle of broken glass and splattered food.

Suddenly dizzy, Sarah slumped to the couch.

Leaning over her, Ken asked, "Sarah . . . you okay? . . . Sarah?"

He tried to rouse her, but she had apparently passed

out. Someone brought over her coat. Ken dressed her limp body and hoisted it up, draping her arm over his shoulder and dragging her out into the fresh air.

Just as he left the front door with the rubber-legged Sarah, the Petersons' car drove up. Mr. Peterson got out of his side of the car and walked over to open Mrs. Peterson's door.

"Ken, is that you?" he asked, straining his eyes in the dark.

"Yes sir," Ken answered as he hurried to get Sarah down the walk and into his car with a minimum of delay.

"What's the trouble?"

"Nothing, just Sarah isn't feeling too well."

Mr. Peterson looked at his wife knowingly.

As they entered the house, they noticed a lot of activity in a corner of the living room. Ray and a few of the kids were busily scraping the food from the carpeting and trying to pick up the pieces of glass. Walking over to the group, Mrs. Peterson, a horrified expression on her face, gasped.

"What's going on?" Her husband ran over to her.

Bending to pick up the pieces, Mrs. Peterson cried, "My favorite lamp."

"Let it go, Grace," Mr. Peterson said, trying to restore order. "They were only having a good time."

He walked into the study and noticed that his bottle of twelve-year-old Scotch was half empty. "Damn kids," he mumbled as he poured himself a drink.

Ken had driven around the block a few times, trying to revive Sarah. He had opened her window, hoping that the cold air would rouse her. She seemed dead to the world. Thinking that a cup of black coffee might help, he drove to the nearest hamburger place. The parking lot was nearly deserted at that time of night.

He bought a cup of coffee, returned to the car, and tried to get Sarah to take a sip.

"Here, drink this."

She opened one glazed eye, struggling to sit up. She accepted the steaming cup, still groggy.

"You ever been to Oregon, Kenny?" she managed to get out.

"Would you drink your coffee?" Ken said forcefully.

"I don't like the taste of coffee." She was petulant.

"Here, put some more sugar in it." He reached over to put in the sugar as she rambled on:

"That's where my daddy's taking me . . . to Oregon. And we're going to have a cabin in the woods. And I'm gonna go to some shacky old high school where they don't have any glee clubs or any other clubs . . ."

Increasingly annoyed by her aimless chatter, Ken shoved the cup to her lips. "C'mon, drink it."

"I don't want to."

"I'm taking you home." He started the motor roughly, turning on his lights.

Sarah pouted in the corner of the seat. "Don't want to . . . don't want to . . ." she mumbled.

They drove up to the Hodges's house, the only house on the street with the lights on. It was 2 A.M.

"Does your stepfather keep a gun?" Ken asked morosely.

"Of course, silly," Sarah perked up. "He's got a teen-age daughter."

"Great," he said as he walked around to help her out of the car.

Sarah walked up the steps to the door, fumbling for the key. Before she could find it, Jean emerged, Matt behind her, both dressed in their bathrobes and looking worn and worried.

"Sarah . . ." Jean's voice was a mixture of concern and anger.

"Hi, Mom. Hi, Matt. This is Ken; he's got a horse."

Extremely upset, Jean put a firm hand on her daughter's shoulder to lead her into the house.

"It's my fault, ma'am." Ken stepped forward, ready to accept the blame. "Y'see . . . some of the kids got to drinking a little, and, well, I convinced Sarah to . . ."

Jean recovered from the shock of Sarah's appearance and completed Ken's sentence. "To go along with the crowd."

"Yes, ma'am. I'm really sorry. It was a dumb thing to do."

But Jean had already maneuvered her stumbling, bleary-eyed daughter into the house.

"All right, mister," Matt said sternly, "you run along. I think you've done enough damage for one night."

"Yes, sir," Ken mumbled, hanging his head in disgrace.

He walked to his car, but his eye was caught by a light in Marsha's window. He could just about see her peering out from behind the curtains. Wearily, he shook his head, climbing into the car.

Having just tucked her barely conscious daughter into bed, Jean returned to her room.

"She okay?" Matt asked.

"I don't know why she isn't throwing up," Jean said, as she climbed into bed beside him. "It worries me that she is so easily led."

"So she had a little to drink," Matt tried to console her. "At least she's not into drugs."

"Yes," Jean said, reaching to turn off the bedside lamp. "Thank God for that."

Chapter Five

The next morning was Sunday, and a disturbed Matt and Jean waited impatiently for Sarah to wake up. Matt idly hit a golf ball into an electric putting cup in the living room. He had wanted to play golf this morning, but Jean had insisted that he wait for Sarah to wake up instead, so that together they could have a word with her about her behavior. Sitting on the couch, Jean absently watched the ball roll into the cup.

"When is that child going to get up?" she scowled.

Rubbing her eyes, Sarah ambled into the living room.

"Hi, everybody," she said cheerfully. "Did I miss breakfast? What time is it, anyhow?"

Jean remained seated, her expression stern.

"It's after eleven. I didn't think you'd be hungry this morning," she said snidely.

"I'm starving," Sarah went on, unaware of her mother's mood. "Is there any bacon left?"

She began to walk into the kitchen, but turned back, suddenly conscious of their indignant stares.

Sinking down into an arm chair, she curled her feet under her green robe. "Oh yeah . . . last night . . . I guess you're not too thrilled about that."

Jean moved toward her daughter. "Should we be?" she asked, standing over her. "Fifteen years old and you come home from a party roaring drunk." She wagged her finger at Sarah.

"I wasn't drunk. I had a couple of tastes."

"I guess I can tell who's drunk and who's not."

"Well, I guess you can," Sarah mimicked. "But at least I didn't puke in the rose bushes, like your friends."

Jean's face colored, and she lashed out at Sarah's impudence by striking her across the face. Sarah's hand went to her reddened cheek, rubbing it gently. Her cheerful expression was replaced by a sullen and beaten look.

Both mother and daughter were ashamed of their behavior, yet neither would renege.

Matt assumed control, stepping over to Jean and putting his arm around her. "We agreed I should handle this, honey." But Matt's attention only served to add fuel to the fire.

"Of all the places to pull a stunt like that—the Petersons'," Jean responded vehemently. "You've embarrassed us. You've made a fool of yourself. In Matt's boss's house."

"Jean, sssh," Matt said, as he walked her over to the couch and sat her down. Then, uncomfortably, he looked at Sarah. "I know I'm not your father. I've never tried to take his place, have I? But I *do* think I have to take some responsibility for handling discipline around here."

Still curled on the chair, Sarah looked at her stepfather reproachfully but gave no sign of answering.

"Now, it seems to me," he continued, "that a boy who gives liquor to a fifteen-year-old girl is not the right kind of boy for you."

"What makes you think it was all *his* fault?" Sarah snapped, challenging.

"Then whose fault is it?" Jean asked.

Sarah looked down at her hands and twisted them.

"Did he give you the liquor or didn't he?"

Sarah still did not answer. She rubbed her hand over the slapped cheek.

"Don't you think your mother's entitled to an answer?" Matt broke in.

Sarah remained silent.

"All right, then." He paced the room, hands behind his back.

Sarah thought he looked even more like an ex-military man than usual.

"I think in this case the punishment—if it's going to mean anything—should give you some time to think about what you've done." He looked at Jean, who gave him an encouraging nod. "So I'm restricting you to quarters for two weeks. No going out. No seeing friends after school. No movies on weekends. Now," he glanced at Sarah who kept her head down, "if that seems unfair, I'd like you to say so.

Tight-lipped, Sarah looked up at him scornfully. "Is the court-martial over?"

"Yes."

"Am I excused?" she asked, getting up from the chair. Then, military-fashion, she turned on her heel and marched out.

"Sarah!" Jean exploded, aghast at her daughter's outright disrespect for Matt.

Spinning around, Sarah looked directly into Jean's eyes. "He's not my father. He's just somebody you sleep with." She ran up to her room, slamming the door.

Jean, horrified, started to cry. Matt comforted her, but he, too, was troubled.

Lying on her bed in the darkening room, Sarah reviewed the day's events. The kids who had been at

Ray's party seemed much more friendly to her today than they had ever been since she started school.

A few had even come up to her.

"You really tied one on Saturday night," Jim, the guitar player, had told her.

His girlfriend had said, "Your folks must have raised hell with you."

"They were going to, but I talked them out of it," Sarah had lied. "I just reminded them of the times I've seen them the same way."

They had both laughed, impressed.

"And it worked?" Jim asked.

"Sure. You should try it."

Their responses had left her feeling that some good had come, after all, from the disastrous night. But Marsha Cooper had seen fit to ruin even that small amount of happiness.

"I just wanted to tell you," she had cornered Sarah in the hall, just before the last class, "I appreciate what you're doing for Kenny."

Sarah looked puzzled.

"Kind of takes the pressure off me, if you know what I mean."

"No, I don't know what you mean."

"Come on," Marsha chided her. "We all know what you were doing in Ken's car until two in the morning."

"Like what?" She eyed Marsha suspiciously.

The bell for the last class sounded, but they both remained fixed, glaring at each other.

"I mean, I understand. A girl whose mother has to fix her up has to give out a little something extra."

Sarah could feel the anger rising.

"Did Ken tell you that?" she demanded.

"Kenny and I have no secrets from each other," Marsha said as she moved away, a self-satisfied smirk on her face.

Now, as Sarah sprawled on her bed, the indignity of Marsha's remarks stung her as if she had been slapped.

She had seen Ken that afternoon but had ignored him, even when he tried to catch up with her after class.

Shifting position, she rolled over on her stomach, picking up a magazine and leafing through it randomly.

Startled, she thought she heard a noise at the window but dismissed it and returned to her magazine. Then she heard it again and decided to investigate.

Raising the window sash, she peered out. Ken motioned for her to come down, but she ignored him, and started to bring the sash down.

"Hey, wait a minute. I'm sorry I got you into trouble. Is that what you're all upset about? Is that why you won't talk to me in school anymore?"

Sarah paused by the window, her hands on the frame.

"That's not the reason," she said quietly.

"Well, what is it?"

She studied him thoughtfully for a moment.

"Marsha. She said that . . ."

"What?" Ken was disturbed. "What did she say?" He tried to read Sarah's expression. "Marsha thinks she owns me." His voice was soft. "But she doesn't."

"That doesn't interest me," Sarah said, straightening up. "I just don't like to go out with boys who make up stories about the girls they ask out."

"What stories?" Ken asked, confused.

"About what we did . . . in your car . . . at two in the morning," Sarah told him hesitantly.

"I never said it, Sarah. Honestly. And if Marsha gives you any more trouble, I'll . . ." he stopped. With a smile he went on, "I'll write her telephone number in every bathroom on campus."

Sarah couldn't help returning his smile.

"Hey, come on out."

Sarah looked at him mournfully. "Can't. I'm grounded for two weeks."

"That's a little heavy, isn't it? I mean half the kids at that party went home loaded."

"My mom didn't think it was so cute."

"Well, maybe if I talk to her . . ."

"Forget it," she cut him off. "Right now she'd rather I go out with a mad rapist."

Ken seemed genuinely upset. "That's too bad. I thought we could maybe go over to the stables. Introduce you to Daisy."

"Daisy?" Sarah was interested.

"My horse. You sure you can't get out on parole?"

"I suppose." Sarah weighed the idea. "I'd have to call Matt at work and confess all my sins. Swear that I'll never do it again. Lay it on real thick. But I think it could work."

"Well, what are you waiting for?"

She reached down and squeezed his hand. "I'll just be a minute. Excited, she ran to the phone and dialed Matt's number. When he got on the phone, she tried to conceal her elation and tone down her voice to sound properly regretful.

"It worked," she yelled to Ken. "Meet you out front."

They got into Ken's car and headed for the stables. On the way, Ken told Sarah about his horse.

"She's old, about eleven. That's why I got her so cheap. But she's still got a lot of good stuff in her. Wait until you see her, you'll love her."

As they pulled into the driveway of the stable, Ken waved to an old white-haired man. "He's the guy who owns this place. Lets me board Daisy real cheap, if I help with some chores."

They got out of the car and walked over the muddy

pathway that led to Daisy's stall. The air reeked of manure and wet hay. Sarah crinkled her nose.

"You'll get used to the smell," Ken said. "It's like perfume to me!"

In her stall, with a red and black plaid blanket over her shoulders, Daisy whinnied at Ken's approach.

"Course, the best part is she loves me. Don't you, Daisy?" He gave her forelock a gentle rub.

The horse nuzzled Ken.

"I think it's terrific that you have something you care that much about," Sarah said as she watched Ken lead Daisy out of her stall and into the corral.

After he had tied Daisy up, he brought out a saddle and bridle. "Wanna go for a ride?"

"Well, I've never been on a horse," Sarah said cautiously.

"That's okay. Daisy won't mind." He led her to the horse slowly.

"I've never even touched a horse before, except ponies when I was a little kid."

"Daisy won't bite. Here, give me your hand." He took it and placed it on Daisy's muzzle.

"It's soft," she said, stroking the horse.

Ken saddled the horse and mounted her. "You coming up here, or do I have to get a rope and pull you up?"

Sarah let him hoist her up in the saddle behind him.

"Don't worry." He turned to look at her frightened face. "I won't let you fall off."

He reined Daisy and led her out of the corral and onto a wooded path.

After they had been riding for a half hour, they reached the beach. Ken gave the horse a slight kick, and it started off into a trot, startling Sarah. She gave a little shriek but was obviously enjoying herself.

Burying her face in his back, she hugged him tighter around the waist.

Ken reined the horse toward the surf, and they trotted through it. Sarah felt light as a bird. Her face was bright, and her long hair flowed behind them like wings.

Bringing Daisy to a stop, Ken swung out of the saddle, landing on the wet sand. "I gotta tell you the truth, Sarah." He stood looking at her for a moment. "When my mom got me to call you, I wasn't too altogether pleased about it, you know what I mean?"

"Sure," Sarah said, looking a little uncomfortable.

"I mean, I thought you were some kind of turkey . . ." He glanced at her with embarrassment. Flustered, he added quickly, "That's not what I mean . . . I . . ."

"That's okay. I guess I sorta was."

"But then at the party you got to singing and coming on kind of kicky. And then you dumped that plate of food all over Marsha's fat chest."

They both laughed at the memory.

Ken went on more seriously. "You're different, Sarah. Different from what I thought you'd be. And different from the other girls around here."

Sarah could feel that Ken's words were not to be taken lightly. She sensed that something deeper was developing between them. He reached up to help her off the horse. As he set her on the ground, he looked at her warmly and brought her closer to him, kissing her softly on the lips. She drew her arms around his neck tightly, holding the kiss a moment longer. They remained together, until Daisy bumped them with her haunches, knocking them to the ground.

Ken playfully threw some sand at Sarah.

"I guess Daisy's jealous, after all," she teased him, running into the waves.

"Another stunt like that, smart-aleck," he told the horse affectionately, "and you're dog meat."

Sarah returned to his side and he put his arm around her. They strolled down the beach, leading Daisy behind them. The sun was setting, and a pink light illuminated the sand and sparkling water. Sarah felt warm and safe, as she had the day she'd been with her father. Maybe, she thought, just maybe, it will be all right after all.

Chapter Six

The blue Camaro drove past the Hodges's house. It screeched to a halt a few houses down. Sarah emerged, carrying her school books. Waving goodbye to Ken, she ran toward her house. What a surprise, she thought, as she let herself in the front door, to find Ken waiting for her after school today, offering to drive her home. She had slipped into the seat beside him, hoping that Marsha had seen her and feeling important.

Entering the dining room, she placed her books on the table.

"I'm home," she called, and began to sift through the mail.

The sound of urgent, muffled voices reached her. She edged closer to the kitchen door and overheard her mother reprimanding Margaret.

"Then who took it, just tell me that? If you didn't take it, who did?"

Sarah inched her way closer; her mother was too involved to notice. They stood by the back door. Margaret's usually cheerful face was marred by lines of worry, and she was trembling slightly. Clutching her purse, Jean looked ill at ease.

"You asked why I'm letting you go. That's why. Now, please let's not make it any more painful than it has to be." She looked up and saw Sarah, a curious expression on her face. "Sarah, nobody asked you to come in here," Jean said.

Margaret spoke, glancing at Sarah for support. "I never touched the liquor, Mrs. Hodges."

"Then what is it I've smelled on your breath? Even today," she said cruelly.

"Sometimes I do," Margaret admitted. "I have a little wine with my lunch. But I didn't think anybody would mind about that."

Sarah could sense that Margaret was covering up for her. They had a mutual bond, an unspoken loyalty. She tried to intercede.

"See, Mom . . . it's all a mistake."

Margaret looked at her imploringly, but Sarah couldn't go on. She didn't want to jeopardize her chances with Matt now that she had apologized to him.

"It's no mistake," Jean contradicted Sarah. And to Margaret, she continued, "My husband says the liquor's been watered down. You can't fool a real Scotch drinker about that. And nobody else has been around here to get into it."

"Then what would it hurt if you gave her another chance?"

But Jean was unresponsive to Sarah's pleas. She handed Margaret some money. "I'm sorry," she said coldly, "but we won't be needing your services any longer."

"Mom, please . . ."

"Do you think a thing like this is easy for me? Do you think I enjoy it?" She pushed the money into Margaret's hand. Margaret accepted it reluctantly. Without looking at either one, Jean pushed by them and said over her shoulder, "I'm meeting Matt for dinner. There's chicken in the refrigerator. We'll be back later."

"Goodbye, Sarah," Margaret told her sadly.

With tears in her eyes, Sarah walked to the window, and watched Margaret trudge pathetically down the driveway. What a coward she was, she realized painfully, letting someone else take the rap for her mistakes. And the tragedy was that Margaret had been her only friend in the entire world, the only person who would take the time to listen to the cries of a lonely girl.

Checking around the corner to make sure that Jean had left, Sarah ran into the den, groping for a bottle and a glass behind the bar. Her hand shook as she held the bottle within inches of the glass. She couldn't pour it, because now they would know, and she couldn't afford their finding out. Reluctantly, she returned the bottle and the glass; she needed another way to get her precious alcohol.

Walking into the kitchen, Sarah looked on her mother's bulletin board for the number of the liquor store.

Cautiously, she dialed the number, placing a tissue over the mouthpiece to disguise her voice. She ordered quickly, her heart beating rigorously inside her chest. Hanging up, she fell into a chair, grabbing herself around the shoulders to stop the shaking. Beads of sweat were forming on her brow; her face had lost all its color. Huddled on the chair, she waited.

It was almost dark when the door bell rang. Sarah ran to open the door.

"Delivery for Mrs. Hodges," a pleasant young man with a red beard announced.

"I'll take it. What is it?" Sarah asked.

"Sorry, pal. Can't leave it with you—it's booze."

"Oh . . ."

"Is your mom here?"

"Sure, come on in," Sarah said, leading him down the hallway toward her mother's room. "She's in the shower."

As they moved down the hallway, they could hear the sound of the shower running. Sarah opened the bathroom door and called above the noise, "Delivery from the liquor store, Mom . . ."

The delivery man took an embarrassed step backward, appearing uncomfortable.

Sarah ducked into the bathroom, shutting the door behind her. Emerging a few seconds later, she said, "She says leave it on the dining table. The money's in her purse."

The young man followed Sarah into the dining room. He removed a fifth of vodka and a half-gallon of cheap wine from the paper sack. "That's eight seventy-three with the tax," he told her. "Of course, I don't know how any grown person can drink this stuff." He pointed to the wine. "Tastes like sugar punch."

"My mom's not too sophisticated," Sarah answered as she handed him a ten-dollar bill which she had taken earlier from Jean's purse. "Keep the change."

"Thanks." He smiled as she let him out the front door.

Sarah remained poised by the front door, until she heard him start the truck. Then she crumbled, her composure giving way to the intensity of her need. She hurried to the bathroom and shut off the empty shower.

Back in the dining room, she gathered up the two bottles and a paper cup and rushed up the stairs to her room. She kicked the door shut with her foot, then put the bottles down on her desk, straining to remove the cap of the vodka bottle. Trembling uncontrollably, she managed to fill the cup with vodka and threw it down her throat. Then, calmly, she filled the cup again, this time with the wine, and set it down on her night table. She went to her closet, hid the bottles beneath the piles of shoes, and closed the door securely.

Settling back on her bed with the pillows propped up behind her, Sarah brought the cup of wine to her lips and sipped it gratefully. The trembling had subsided, and she felt peaceful. She had forgotten all about Marsha and her lies; Margaret's dismissal; her father's absence. Feeling light and carefree, she floated above all her problems, as they slowly lost all meaning and disappeared.

Chapter Seven

Each morning it was becoming more difficult for Sarah to get up. When she awoke at seven, she was always in a fog, her head cloudy. Getting dressed and making it downstairs for breakfast was an ordeal. When she finally wandered into school, she was shaking and weak. She had tried to solve this dilemma by always carrying in her bag a cologne bottle filled with vodka. This way, she would never be too far from relief.

Rushing down the hall, Sarah tried to get to her locker before she was caught out of class without a pass. Clutching a can of apple juice with a straw in it, she reached her locker, fumbled with the combination, and opened it. She grabbed the cologne bottle which she had transferred from her bag to her locker and poured the clear liquid into the can.

"You taken to drinking cologne now?" a familiar voice asked.

Surprised, Sarah spun around, hiding the bottle behind her back.

"You know it's not very nice to sneak up on a person," she said to the smiling, concerned face of Ken. She quickly re-capped the bottle, put it back in the locker, reached for her books, and left the apple juice behind.

"Could I taste that?" Ken asked as she slammed the door shut.

"What are you," she wondered lightly, trying to make a joke, "a cop or something?"

"You sure turned onto that stuff in a pretty fast hurry."

"What time's the beach party Saturday night?" Sarah asked, avoiding his eyes. "Are we gonna drive or take Daisy?"

Ken leaned back against the locker door and pursed his lips thoughtfully. "Sarah, you've got me a little worried." He put his hand on her shoulder. "Don't you think drinking in school—I mean right here in the hall—don't you think that's a little dumb?"

She shook off his hand, recoiling from the words.

"And don't you think you're being a little square? Go out to the lunch court and check the thermoses—half of them smell from sour mash." She shifted her books in her arms and fired off the words: "It's not such a major crime!"

"I just don't like to see you doing it."

"Well, remember," she said demurely, "you're the one who got me started."

"Am I?" Ken demanded sharply.

Suddenly on the defensive, Sarah reverted to her sweet and innocent act.

"Okay, Kenny. I'm sorry," she looked up at him shyly. "You don't want me to, I won't do it anymore."

Ken started to respond, but he noticed a girl rushing toward Sarah with a piece of pink paper in her hand.

"I've been looking all over for you," she said, out of breath. "They want to see you in Farrell's office."

"Me? What for?" She looked at Ken anxiously.

"I don't know," the girl said, "but you'd better haul it on over there—your mother's in with her now."

Distracted, Sarah started to move away, but then she turned to face Ken.

"You'll call me?"

He nodded and walked off in the other direction.

Sarah took a few seconds to compose herself. She was very apprehensive. She popped a breath mint into her mouth, and then another. Straightening her collar and patting her hair in place, she headed toward the vice-principal's office, expecting the worst.

Mrs. Farrell was a pleasant-mannered woman in her late forties, with brown, straight hair styled in a page-boy. Behind her thick glasses were friendly gray eyes. Although she was the vice-principal of girls, she was also known as an interested listener to all students' problems.

She ushered Sarah into her office, where Jean had been sitting for half an hour. Mother and daughter gave each other annoyed looks. Jean was especially irritated at having been called away from her bridge game.

"I think you know what the problem is, Sarah," Mrs. Farrell said in a soft, soothing voice. "You've been cutting classes."

Sarah looked at her mother for support.

"I told Mrs. Farrell there's been a mistake and you would clear it up," Jean said drily.

Both women waited for Sarah to reply. Her palms started to sweat, and her mind raced through hundreds of excuses.

After a minute, she said: "Well . . . uh . . . last week a couple of times . . . I had to go to the library for this report I'm doing on overpopulation . . . and last Thursday I got my . . . you know . . . my period, and I just went to a friend's car to lie down for a little while. . . ."

Mrs. Farrell looked dismayed. "Why didn't you go to the nurse's office?"

"I guess I should have . . . Mom, it was a mistake. It only happened a couple of times. Tell her you said it was okay."

Tight-lipped, Jean only glared at her daughter.

Reaching into her desk drawer, Mrs. Farrell brought out two handwritten notes. Sarah blanched at the sight of them.

"Is this your signature on these absence excuses, Mrs. Hodges?" She pushed the notes across her desk.

Jean studied them for a moment and then shook her head grimly, pushing the notes back. There was a moment of deadly silence.

"It's almost time for your class, Sarah." Mrs. Farrell was the first to speak. "You run along. Your mother and I will try to sort this out."

Sarah started to go but looked back at Jean mournfully.

"Go on," Mrs. Farrell urged.

Pushing wildly past students pouring out from their classrooms, Sarah finally arrived at her locker. She tore the lock off the door and reached for the can of spiked apple juice. Without even checking to see if anyone was around, she threw her head back and gulped down the gin.

In the vice-principal's office, Jean was just getting up to leave.

"You've made your point," she said as she put on her coat. "Now it's up to me, isn't it?"

But Mrs. Farrell continued to read, in a monotone, from Sarah's file: ". . . refuses to undress for gym . . . seems distracted . . . mediocre grades . . . just enough to get by." She closed the file, took off her glasses, and looked at Jean earnestly. "Mrs. Hodges, Sarah is a child with a high I.Q. And a lot of potential. Something's wrong."

"It's a new school situation," Jean replied blandly. What did this stranger know about her personal problems, she thought. They were none of *her* business.

"I also have Sarah's record here from her last school."

Jean couldn't stand a minute more of this woman's chattering. She started for the door. "I'll have Mr. Hodges talk to her as soon as he gets home this evening."

"I'm not sure that's the answer," Mrs. Farrell said to Jean, who looked as if she were ready to pounce on her.

Motioning for Jean to sit down again, Mrs. Farrell continued in a clinical tone. "She has trouble fitting in. Her moods are erratic; she often seems depressed."

"She's a teenager; teenagers are like that. I used to get depressed if I got a pimple on my chin." She hadn't asked for all this professional hogwash. Her daughter was depressed; a normal, healthy depressed teenager.

But Mrs. Farrell was not easily stopped. "Last year we had a boy who was depressed over a mild case of acne. He hanged himself." She let the words sink in.

"But there must have been something else wrong with him!" Jean said, shocked.

"Not necessarily. Some kids just handle things better than others. His parents felt it was just a phase he was going through." She pushed back her chair and approached Jean solicitously.

"Maybe some professional counseling could help."

"I don't think so," Jean said, totally against the idea. Why was this woman taking a typical situation and turning it into a melodrama?

"The records show that you were remarried less

than two years ago," Mrs. Farrell went on, trying a different angle.

Stirred up by the woman's prying, Jean retorted violently: "That's right. And do the records also show the kind of man I married? He's decent, hardworking. He tries to be a positive influence on my daughter."

"Mrs. Hodges," Mrs. Farrell tried to calm her down, "I didn't mean to imply . . ."

"Has anybody bothered to put in the records that I've managed—somehow—to raise another daughter? Who's happily married and has a new baby." Her voice rose an octave. "And who never tried to hang herself."

Jean jumped to her feet, her hand on the doorknob. "I don't know about you people. You gotta believe every kid from a divorced home is a candidate for nine years on a psychiatrist's couch. That's it, isn't it? Well, maybe if the school did its job—made learning a little more interesting, got rid of distractions . . . Maybe if you did that, instead of pulling out the dime-store psychology everytime you have a simple discipline problem . . ."

Mrs. Farrell observed Jean silently, letting her blow off steam. Jean, aware that she was becoming irrational, suddenly stopped and composed herself.

"Well, even if *you* don't, my husband knows how to handle this sort of thing," she said as she left the office, closing the door firmly behind her.

Upset by her encounter with Mrs. Farrell, Jean hurried through the hall and into the parking lot. She got in the car, turned on the ignition, and pulled out, heading for home. She would have to speak to Matt about Sarah. This couldn't go on. It must be the crowd she's hanging around with. What ever possessed her to fix Sarah up with that boy Ken Newkirk, Jean thought, frowning. It's all his fault;

he's a bad influence on Sarah. She'd have to tell Matt to extend Sarah's punishment. A few more days in solitary would do her good.

Instead of taking the turn that led to her neighborhood, Jean pulled over to the side of the road and made a call to Matt from a telephone booth. She asked him to meet her for drinks; they'd discuss Sarah over cocktails.

Sarah had decided to go home, rather than attend her last class. Even the gin in her cologne bottle did little to settle the uneasy feeling that was invading her. She didn't know why she was depressed and unhappy; she just was. She tried to cheer herself up with the thought that she was going to a party with Ken, but even that did no good. She always felt she was on the verge of losing him anyway, and she was nervous and unsure of herself when she was around him. Of course, she couldn't bring herself to discuss these feelings with her mother. A wall had been erected between them ever since the divorce, and each day only added another stone to that wall. And, besides, Sarah thought tearfully, Jean had Matt and now Nancy's new baby to think about. Sarah was too much of a bother for her. Sarah was beginning to hate the four walls of her room. She didn't do her homework or read. She didn't do anything but lie on her back and stare at the ceiling. Occcassionally, she would flip through a magazine, some of which were now strewn haphazardly about the floor. She wanted to leave her parents' house, their neighborhood, run off to Oregon. She wanted to be free from their pressure to fit in with the crowd.

At the sound of the door bell, Sarah jumped up and ran downstairs to the bathroom to turn on the shower. She opened the door to the delivery man, but he was different from the one before; much older and sterner-looking.

"Just a minute," Sarah told him over her shoulder as she went to the bathroom door to call out: "Delivery from the liquor store, Mom. What do you want me to do about it?"

She led him into the dining room and had him place the bottles on the table. They were the same as before —a fifth of vodka and a half-gallon of wine. "How much is that?" Sarah asked, reaching into her purse for the money.

"I'll just wait for your mother to come out, if you don't mind." A slight, balding man, he spoke deliberately.

"Sure, I don't mind," she said, squirming slightly.

Then, forcing a smile, she continued: "Course, my mother's one of the long shower-takers of Western civilization. We're thinking of getting her into the *Guinness Book of World Records.*"

The man looked unperturbed. "That's the advantage of being the boss—I have all the time in the world."

Realizing that she was caught, Sarah tried to stall for a few minutes, glancing around the room to see if her mother was coming.

Then, "Look, mister," she admitted grudgingly, "I'll tell you the truth, okay? My mother's not home."

"I know," he said quietly.

"See, it's my dad's birthday, and I wanted to surprise him with . . ." She was pleased with her lie, but the owner gave her an incredulous look.

"If you tell my mom about this," she stammered, becoming frightened, "I'm in real trouble."

"Look, honey," the owner warned her, "If I'd left this stuff with you, *I* could be in real trouble. I could have lost my license."

"I'm sorry," Sarah said, genuinely upset, "I didn't think about that."

She was trapped now; an animal in a snare. If she didn't have a drink soon, she would explode. She could feel her body giving way. The shaking would start soon and then the terrible sweating. If he didn't give her those bottles, she didn't know what would happen.

"What time do you expect your mother back?"

"Please, mister . . ." Sarah cried desperately.

He looked at her solemnly and then patted her on the head. "All right. I'm gonna let you off this once. But if you ever try a stunt like this again . . ." He started to pick up the bottles and put them back into the bag. Sarah stared at them hungrily, her eyes wide and her face chalk-white.

"I won't," she barely mumbled. "Honest. Thank you . . . thanks a lot."

She watched him walk out the front door and close it gently behind him. "You bastard," she mouthed, as she threw herself on the living room couch. The shaking was uncontrollable now. Her teeth were chattering, and she felt as if her whole head were about to burst. Sitting up, she wrapped her arms around her shoulders tightly to prevent the trembling, but she couldn't stop. Despairing, she let the tears fall.

Chapter Eight

Nancy had always been their mother's favorite. Sarah could remember worshipping her older sister from afar as Nancy would get ready for a date. She had always been prettier than Sarah, better at school, and more popular with the boys. And, it seemed to Sarah that Jean had spent all her love on Nancy and had none left to give to her younger daughter.

Sarah, on the other hand, was her father's favorite, sharing with him all his treasured pastimes—going to baseball games; taking long walks on the beach; fishing; appreciating the beauty in nature. Jerry had left Sarah a legacy of important, wonderful heirlooms. Not having him around, she felt alone and deserted.

"Did you ever want me to be a boy?" Sarah would often ask her father.

"No, never," Jerry would tell her tenderly, "I like you just the way you are."

Following in her mother's footsteps, Nancy had married young, barely twenty, and had finished only two years of college. She had passed up a career as a biologist to marry Ted Stewart. Jean had encouraged the match, feeling that Ted, an engineer, had a "good future." Consequently, Nancy gave up her life-long dream of being biologist for "security" and a baby.

The birth of Laurie had brought the two sisters

closer. They were seven years apart and had never
been intimates. Laurie was their common denominator.
Sarah enjoyed going to Ted and Nancy's pleasant
garden apartment, which was not far from the
Hodges's home. She used it as an escape from her
parents and from school.

"She loves it," Nancy said to a beaming Sarah, who
was holding up a colorful mobile.

"She should," Sarah said, looking down fondly at
the baby. "Her aunt made it for her in prison."

They were in the yellow and white nursery that
Nancy had painstakingly decorated, and Sarah was
standing on a chair hanging the mobile. It was Saturday, and Sarah had come over in the morning to
watch Laurie while Nancy shopped. Sarah loved the
time she spent with the infant, who, at three months,
was just beginning to become aware of the world
around her. Although she was asleep most of the time,
Sarah was always at her side, arranging the blanket,
making sure that she was comfortable. Wondering
whether she would ever have a husband or a child,
Sarah would sit in a rocking chair by the crib and
hum softly to Laurie, imagining that she were her
child.

Nancy finished diapering Laurie and put her down
for a nap, motioning for Sarah to follow her out of
the room.

"I'd say you got off easy," Nancy told her as they
settled themselves in the den. "Aren't they letting you
go to the beach party?" The afternoon sunlight flooded
through the curtained windows. Jean had helped Nancy
decorate, and the room retained many of Jean's
touches; an Indian patterned rug, a leather couch,
some fur throw pillows grouped around a few potted
plants. Sarah wished they had stayed in the nursery,

where she felt more secure, more distant from her mother's dominance.

"Yeah, big deal." Sarah hoped Nancy took her edginess for excitement about the party. She really needed a drink now; the pressure of the upcoming evening was upon her.

"Who are you going with?" Nancy asked.

"Just some kids."

"No special boy?"

Sarah picked up a pillow and held it to her chest. "Not really."

"Hey, c'mon," Nancy urged. "What are big sisters for?"

"Well . . ."

"Is he cute? Is he tall?"

Blushing, Sarah poured her heart out. "He's just about the most super guy in school. I mean, can you believe a guy like that is interested in me"

"Why shouldn't he be?" Nancy inquired, walking into the kitchen and putting some soft drinks and glasses on a tray. She noticed that the door to the liquor cabinet was open and absently pushed it closed with her foot.

"You got three days? I'll list all the reasons."

"I'm surprised Mom hasn't mentioned this to me."

Aware immediately of her mistake, Sarah tried to cover up. Now she knew she couldn't trust her sister.

"Mom hasn't met him yet," she hedged.

"Doesn't he come by the house to pick you up?"

"No, he . . . uh . . . doesn't live nearby. He goes to a different school."

"You said he goes to your school." Nancy was getting annoyed at Sarah's evasion of the subject.

"Sarah," she said, sounding more like Jean than the young woman she was, "you're not talking about that creep who got you drunk that night? Ken what's-his-name?"

Resentful at Nancy's cross-examination, Sarah paced across the room. "He's not a creep," she said stubbornly. "He's not like that, honest. It wasn't his fault." She looked at Nancy frantically. "You're not going to tell Mom, are you?"

Sarah kneeled at Nancy's side. " 'What are big sisters for?' you said," she repeated, imploringly. "Promise you won't tell."

Nancy didn't answer but seemed to weigh the consequences.

"Promise," Sarah was practically begging. "Please."

"Okay," Nancy said reluctantly. "I promise."

"I think I'm going to go now." Sarah gathered her coat and books.

But Nancy was not going to let the subject drop that easily.

"But why can't you just tell Mom? Why can't you be straight with her? She'll understand."

Sarah laughed sardonically at her sister's last remark.

"She won't. She never has. It seems like all I ever do is embarrass her." She paused. "Sometimes I think she doesn't like me very much."

"I swear, you sound more like Daddy every day."

"I'm beginning to understand what Daddy had to live through," Sarah said with uncharacteristic maturity.

"What about her?" Nancy was disturbed by Sarah's statement. "What about what Mom had to live through? Sarah, believe me, you weren't old enough to know what was going on between them."

Agitated and jumpy, Sarah was practically screaming: "Oh, yes I was. He was an artist, and she squeezed all the life and all the joy out of him. Like he was some old tube of gray paint. And she turned him into a . . . a . . . salesman."

"He was a dreamer," Nancy said, soothingly. "And she tried to turn him into a husband. Is that so wrong?"

Troubled, Sarah whispered, "Yes." And then louder and more forceful, "Yes, yes . . ."

She stormed into Nancy's kitchen, grabbing her shoulder bag from the counter and tearing out the back door. Nancy, a hurt look on her face, followed her.

"Sarah, wait," she called, but Sarah was already on her bicycle, pedaling furiously.

Sarah wanted to get as far away from Nancy and her mother as possible. They were cut from the same cloth; they only wanted to mold her into their image, to destroy her uniqueness and anything that reminded them of Jerry. She rode frantically, making sure that the half-empty gin bottle that she had stolen from Nancy was securely stashed in her bag.

Exhausted, Sarah had ridden her bicycle all day until it was time to go home and get ready for the beach party. She wanted to look especially nice for Ken and had taken extra pains to wash and set her hair the night before.

She left a half hour before the party was to begin in order to meet Ken at the stables. He was standing by Daisy's stall, and he gave Sarah a warm welcome as she walked up. Still upset from her argument with Nancy that afternoon, Sarah tried to hide her feelings from Ken. They mounted the horse and headed for the beach. As they were waiting to cross the highway, the horse shied.

"Easy, horse." Ken reined her in. He turned back to Sarah. "Lights made her nervous."

They crossed the highway and followed the glow to the big bonfire on the beach. A full moon was shining on the kids clustered around the fire and a few guitarists. A gentle surf washed up along the shore. Its melody could be heard in the background.

Ken tied Daisy to a bush and gave her some leaves to munch on. Then Ken and Sarah walked hand in hand toward the fire.

"Special treat for tonight," Ray's familiar voice boomed out.

"Up to his old tricks again?" Ken wondered as they watched him carry a huge watermelon to a blanket and proceed to poke holes in the melon with an ice pick. Sticking straws into the holes, he motioned for everyone to gather around him.

"What's that for?" Sarah asked as she watched the others.

"It's Ray's famous watermelon trick. He plugs the thing and pours in about a quart and a half of gin."

Brightening, Sarah sauntered off toward the group around the watermelon. "No kidding . . ."

Ken followed her, conscious of a change in her mood. Hardly able to keep up with her, he ran over to where the kids, Sarah included, were squirming on their bellies around the melon, like nursing kittens.

"Hey Sarah," someone called, "leave a little for the rest of us orphans."

Leaning over to tap her on the shouder, Ken noticed the vigor with which Sarah was sucking on the straw. It was as if her very life depended on it! Frightened, he nudged her, but she didn't respond. He tapped her again, harder.

"Sarah . . . could I talk to you?"

Straining to pull herself away from the melon, Sarah complied. Ken grabbed her hand roughly and pulled her over to a secluded area away from the fire. Sarah pouted, huddled by a tree. Ken, his face serious, chastised her: "I thought you told me you were going to stop. You promised me that day in the hall that you were going to stop."

"Why do you have to get on me too? I get enough of that with my mother."

"Why do you have to lie? I never expected that from you, Sarah."

"Lie about what?" She looked at him narrowly, wishing that he would let up on this discussion and allow her to return to the watermelon.

"About drinking. About that I got you started. Letting me take the blame that first night."

Shaken by his words, Sarah spoke in a small voice. "Oh, that . . ."

"You don't drink like a beginner," Ken continued in a paternal tone.

"Well, I'm glad you know. Because I've felt so rotten about that. But if my Mom ever . . ."

"I don't care about taking the blame."

"You don't?" Sarah asked softly.

He looked at her closely for a few seconds. Her upturned face was so tender, so young. He felt as if he were years older than she.

"I care about you," he said in a compassionate voice. She edged closer, but he held her back. He wasn't saying the words for effect; he really meant them, and he wanted Sarah to believe in them, too.

"I care that you seem to need the stuff."

Sensing that Ken was serious, Sarah tried to lighten the discussion.

"Oh come on, Ken," she said flippantly." You make me sound like some major alcoholic freak." He remained quiet, contemplating her. She went on: "I don't see giant purple cockroaches crawling up the wall, you know." Frustrated at his silence, she became more enraged. "I take a drink once in a while because it makes me feel good, okay? It makes the hassles about my folks and school and all that tacky stuff—it just makes it all go down a little easier."

"Then why do you hav*e* to drink when you're with me?"

"I don't *have* to drink at all. I could stop any time I feel like it. I just don't feel like it."

After all these months, Sarah was relieved finally to discuss her problem with someone. It had been painful to keep all her anguish inside, to hide her true feelings from the world. She wanted to reach out and touch Ken, to experience the closeness of another person. She didn't want to be alone any more.

Ken roused her from her thoughts. "Let's go back to the fire."

"Let's not," Sarah said, warming to him.

"Why?"

"Let's not, because . . ." She leaned against him, her whole body aching for his embrace. Longing to be recognized as a person with desires, fears, hopes, she whispered in his ear, "If you want me to stop, I'll stop."

He studied her somberly. Slowly, she reached up and put her arms around his neck. She drew his head down to hers and kissed him, hungrily, on the mouth. He didn't resist but returned her caress. Pressed together, they sank to the sand. Sarah gave a little cry. "Hush," Ken whispered, "it's all right."

Chapter Nine

The light from the television set was reflected off the intent faces of Matt and Jean. Matt was settled comfortably in an arm chair with his feet up, a can of beer in his hand. Jean, on the couch, was occupied with her needlepoint.

Both were still very upset about the meeting with Mrs. Farrell although they hadn't agreed on the best course of action. Matt felt that Sarah should have another chance to prove herself. He had never had any children of his own; in fact, he had never been married before. A career army officer for twenty-five years, he had found no time for the amenities of married life.

He had met Jean at a cocktail party given by mutual friends and was as taken by the soft-spoken, well-dressed, sophisticated woman as she was by him.

Matt Hodges was the antithesis of Jerry Travis. While Matt was tall and fair, Jerry was short and dark; he was ambitious, while Jerry was a dreamer; he was a doer, while Jerry was a thinker. When Jean first met Matt, her marriage to Jerry had been deteriorating to such a point that they practically led separate lives.

Because of Matt's technical skill in the field of electronics and his vast administrative abilities gleaned from a quarter century of army life, he was pursued by a number of prestigious companies, Peterson's among them. While, Matt, on the other hand, pursued Jean.

He wooed her like a school boy, sending her flowers and candy. And she fell for him as if he were her first crush. They were married only two days after her divorce from Jerry became final.

When Peterson had recently offered Matt the vice-presidency of his electronics firm, Matt felt the time was ripe, and he moved Jean and Sarah to their present home. Married two years, the intensity that Matt and Jean experienced when they first met had not faded. Unfortunately, they had not been able to communicate or share that love with Sarah. She, of all the players in the game, was to suffer the most.

Entering the partially lighted room, Sarah went to the window and pulled back the curtains to look outside. She had her coat on and was carrying a stack of books.

"Babysitting tonight?" Matt wondered.

"Uh huh."

"What are you going to do with all that money you're making?"

"I'll think of something," Sarah answered arrogantly.

Matt believed in training children as one would train a dog. Not that he meant to be cruel or unjust, but he believed in a system of reward and punishment in order to instill in a child the proper respect for authority. He felt that Jerry had failed miserably to instill this respect in Sarah. But he felt that she had served her recent punishment—remaining in her room after school for two weeks—like a true soldier, and he was proud of her. Now he was willing to make amends.

"There's a sale on TV sets at Gorton's. I was just thinking, I'd be willing to match whatever you've got. How'd you like to have a new color set?"

Sarah was taken aback by Matt's sudden interest in her and was pleased by his attention.

"Really?"

"Sure."

"That'd be super," she said, genuinely happy.

"Okay." He got up and walked into the kitchen for another beer. "Let's talk about it later."

Hearing a horn outside, Sarah ran to the door. "That's for me. Night, Matt. See you later, Mom."

Jean, as an afterthought, called to her. "Oh, by the way, your father called today. He asked me to tell you he's sorry . . . but he won't be in this weekend."

Sarah paused by the door and faced Jean, disappointment straining her face.

"Maybe you and Matt and I could . . ." Jean offered but stopped at Sarah's reaction.

"I'm sure he has a good reason," Sarah recovered quickly. "Probably that new job . . . that big new job he was waiting to hear about."

The horn sounded again, and Sarah ran out, forcing the tears back. She got into the waiting car. Fred Tyler, in his early thirties, leaned over to open the door for her. Officious and cold, Fred Tyler didn't particularly like Sarah nor she him. But she loved to watch his two-year-old son Luke.

"Mr. Tyler," she asked hesitantly, "is it okay if I have a friend over to study with me?"

"I don't see why not," Fred Tyler replied perfunctorily. He dropped her off in front of his house and honked the horn impatiently. His wife, a meek, mousy woman, came scampering out. He must be an efficiency expert, Sarah thought whimsically. Everything's running like clockwork.

Sarah was in a fairly good mood, especially since Ken was going to keep her company. And Matt's sudden interest in her was an unexpected surprise. She only wished that Jean would spend more time with her. They hadn't discussed the scene in Mrs. Farrell's office, and Sarah was suspicious of her mother's silence. She would rather Jean scream and rant than keep it inside and let it brew.

She heard a knock on the back door and let Ken in. He seemed preoccupied, not his usually loose self.

"What's the matter?" Sarah asked.

"Nothing except that I have a huge chemistry exam on Monday, and if I don't study for it, I'm going to flunk!"

"Well, I won't bother you," Sarah told him. "I won't even open my mouth. I wouldn't want you to flunk your test on *my* account."

"C'mon, don't take it personally." He sat down at the kitchen table and spread out his textbooks and notebooks.

Sarah went into the baby's room to make sure that he was all right. Luke lay curled in a corner of his crib, sucking his thumb. His eyes fluttered open slightly, and he gave Sarah a sleepy smile. She tucked him in and crept out of the room.

Her math book opened before her, Sarah had tried to study but was having trouble concentrating. She and Ken had not discussed the night of the beach party, and she had many unanswered questions floating around in her head. She felt as if she had made an enormous commitment to him, and she wanted some feedback, some recognition that his feelings were the same. It had been her first sexual experience, and she was both confused and elated. It had all happened so quickly, not at all the way she had imagined, and she felt at once thrilled and scared.

"Ken?" she asked timidly, reaching over to tap him lightly on the hand. He looked up, annoyed at the disturbance, and then went back to his books. She went on. "The other night on the beach . . ."

"Yeah?" he said without looking up.

"It was kind of special," she said, her eyes brightening as she recalled the moment.

"It was for me too," he said softly.

"I mean, I'd never . . . *you* know . . ."

He smiled at her openly. "Me neither."

"That's what I thought," Sarah told him, smiling in spite of herself. He returned to his studying. She let a few minutes pass, but couldn't contain herself. "Why aren't we . . ." she continued shyly, "you know . . . going together?"

He looked up, astonished at her frankness, and shrugged.

"We're just not."

"Then why don't we?"

"I thought the guy was supposed to ask the girl that."

Stung by his rejection, Sarah sat back in her chair, hands in her lap. Hassled, Ken returned to his books, ignoring her presence. She was not satisfied with his answers and felt the need to pursue the conversation. "I haven't had a drink since the beach party," she told him proudly.

"Good," he replied drily.

Frustrated by his disinterest, Sarah leaped from her chair, scattering her papers all over the floor.

"Is that all you can say—'good'?"

"You said you weren't a booze freak." He was calm. "I believed you."

"How come you didn't call me until last night?" She sat down and studied him.

"Sarah," he said, impatient with her insistent, demanding tone. "If I don't get at least a B in chemistry, I can kiss veterinary college good-bye. So let's just do our homework, okay?"

Confused and disturbed by his insensitivity, Sarah sat at the table, biting her hand nervously. She knew that if she said one more word, it would upset him; but she couldn't keep quiet, she couldn't keep the words inside of her any longer.

"I love you, Ken," she blurted out.

Her words touched him, not because he felt the same way as she did—he didn't know how he felt about her. He honestly hadn't given her much thought. But he was struck by the desperation, the loneliness, the pathetic sound of her words. He stared at her blankly.

"Do you love me?" she repeated. "Well, do you?"

"Isn't that kind of heavy? We've only known each other a few weeks."

But Sarah felt no restraint.

"Not if we feel it."

"I like things the way they are. It's been good so far. Why do you want to push?" Ken replied.

Distraught, Sarah responded frantically. "You love your dumb horse—you don't keep that any secret." She gripped the edge of the table, her face reddening.

"Sarah, that's stupid—Daisy isn't a person."

Rising suddenly, she threw her chair back and paced the room. "I'm sorry if you think I'm stupid."

Patiently, Ken got up from his chair and walked over to her, taking her by the shoulders. He could feel how tense and pent-up she was, as if she were ready to explode.

"I like you, Sarah." He paused, sighing with the weight of his admission, and went on. "I maybe even like you better than any other girl. But that doesn't mean . . ."

Sarah spun around, knocking off his hands.

"What other girl?" she asked accusingly.

"You know . . ."

"I don't know. Have you ben seeing other girls?"

"Well, sure . . . some." She had cornered him, and he was faltering under her interrogation.

"Why?" she asked, feeling betrayed. "I haven't been seeing other boys."

"We never had that kind of understanding."

"Who?" she demanded, her voice rising. "Marsha? Have you been seeing her?"

"Hey," Ken broke in sharply. "I don't need this."

Breathing hard, her face red and her eyes wild, Sarah was on the verge of hysteria. "I should have known. I should have known you were only . . ." she sobbed and gasped for air, ". . . using me!"

Turning from Ken, Sarah tried to control her flood of tears. Stricken, she noticed that the baby was in the room, silently absorbing their quarrel. "Now look what you've done," she accused. She picked up the whimpering child, still sniffling herself.

"I think maybe I'd better go," Ken told her somberly.

"I think that's a terrific idea," she said, carrying the baby into the living room. "Go on back to your Marsha," she called over her shoulder as Ken moved toward the door. "Go tell her what a fool I've been." She turned her back disdainfully, telling herself she didn't need him, she didn't care . . .

At the sound of the door slamming, Sarah's face creased with pain, and she rushed to the door. "Kenny, I didn't mean it," she called in vain. "Kenny, come back."

She heard his car pulling away and felt the walls of the room closing in, the lights blinking around her. She held onto the wall for support. The baby, held in her other arm, sensed her anguish and started to cry.

"Now what am I going to do" she asked the child. "Okay. Okay. I'll get your bottle."

Holding Luke tightly, she entered the kitchen and rummaged through the refrigerator, looking for his milk. Her eye fell on a full bottle of wine. She grabbed the baby's bottle, closing the door of the refrigerator, but the image of the unopened wine sitting on the shelf would not leave her mind.

She carried the baby to his room, put him down in his crib, and gave him his bottle, which he accepted gratefully. She stood there while he finished the milk. Then, his hunger satisfied, he rolled over onto his stomach and fell asleep.

In the den, Sarah tried her father's telephone number. She was shaking, exhausted, emotionally drained. She had to hear her father's voice, his reassuring, comforting voice. He was all that mattered to her in the world. Let down by her mother, and now by Ken, all she had left was her father.

"Please . . ." she implored the operator, "he's got to be there." She let the phone ring a long time, clinging to it forlornly, cradling it like a baby. Then, slowly, painfully, she hung up.

"Daddy . . . Daddy," she whispered tearfully, moving uncontrollably toward the kitchen.

The Tylers arrived home at one in the morning. Fred Tyler walked to the front door and reached into his pocket. Embarrassed, he looked at his wife.

"Damn. Forgot my house key. You bring yours?"

She shook her head. They rang the door bell, gently so as not to wake their child, and waited. No one answered. Fred rang it again, with more force. Still no answer. Now he rang the bell hard and pounded on the door. His wife stood beside him, paralyzed with fear. She could hear her child crying helplessly in the background.

Without a moment's hesitation, Fred ran around to the back of the house and to the French windows of the den. He shattered the glass with his fist, stuck his hand through, and pulled open the door from the other side.

Sarah lay in a crumpled heap on the floor. An empty wine bottle stared at the distraught and disgusted parents. Mrs. Tyler rushed to her child, who was sobbing as if he had been crying for hours.

"Sarah?" Fred shook her roughly. "Come on, get up."

She opened one eye tentatively and then closed it. The room was spinning around her; she didn't know where she was or who the strange man was standing over her.

"Come on, miss." He grabbed her arms and swung her over his shoulder. "I'm taking you home."

He maneuvered the limp body into the front seat of his car and furiously drove to her home. He slammed on the brakes in front of the Hodges's houses and stormed up to the door. Matt was already there when he got to the front stoop.

"What's going on? What's the matter?"

"Your daughter." Fred Tyler pointed to the car. "She's dead drunk. Get her out of my car."

Matt rushed down the front steps and blanched when he saw Sarah, her clothes in disarray, passed out on the front seat.

"How'd this happen?" he demanded of Tyler as he pulled his stepdaughter out of the car and carried her into the house.

"That's the last time she sets foot in my house. I found her drunk on the floor with my kid crying his eyes out for God-knows-how-long. You better watch that girl, Hodges, she's in for big trouble."

They propped her up on the couch, and Jean washed her face with cold water and tried to pour black coffee down her throat. Sarah spat it out. Finally, after ten minutes, she was able to sit up.

Jean was in a fury. "You're just lucky Fred Tyler didn't call the police. Do you know that? This is going to be all over the neighborhood. It's going to be all over Matt's office." She shook her daughter by the shoulders. "Just what was in your mind when you decided to pull such a stupid stunt?"

Ashamed, Sarah tried to pull away from her mother's grip, but Jean held her face between her hands.

"Answer me! Don't you have anything to say?"

Sarah looked up into her mother's face woefully and whispered, "I think I'm going to be sick."

Jean pushed away Sarah's face with loathing. She walked to the other side of the room and gloated: "Good. I hope you get so hung over you're in bed for a week." Her voice was pinched and tight. "Maybe that'll give you something to think about next time."

Sarah tried to get up to go to the bathroom, but Jean pushed her back down on the couch.

"Sit there," she glared. "Did *he* get drunk too?"

"Who?" Sarah asked weakly.

"You know who. That Ken character. And don't bother telling me you haven't been seeing him because I know otherwise." Jean presented her with the irrefutable evidence.

"Did Nancy tell you that?" Sarah, dumfounded at her sister's betrayal, cried, "She promised . . ."

"Never mind who told me—it was for your own good."

Matt, who had remained in the background, stepped forward calmly.

"I told you, Jean—last week—what had to be done. Now do you agree with me?"

Jean nodded, giving Sarah a hostile glance.

Matt walked over to the phone directory and started to look up a number. Sarah, realizing what he was doing, jumped to her feet, terrified, but helpless against the both of them.

"What? What has to be done? Who are you calling?"

"His parents," Matt said with a severity that Sarah hadn't heard before.

"Matt's going to tell them to keep that son of theirs away from my daughter. That he's got her drinking and God-knows-what else."

"Don't!" Sarah pleaded, full of humiliation and shame. "Don't call. Ken had nothing to do with my drinking." If her parents called and confronted him, it would be all over. She could handle their anger but not his. If only he hadn't left in such a state, she could reach him, warn him. She looked mournfully at her mother.

"Don't try to protect him, Sarah. It won't work." Jean was by the phone, urging Matt to dial.

Her moment of truth had come; she had to tell them everything, admit honestly and truthfully what she had been hiding for almost two years. She couldn't bring herself to do it, but so much depended on her decision. Sitting on the couch, breathing deeply, she began: "You remember after the Christmas party when I got so sick, and the doctor said it must have been a stomach flu?" She looked at Matt and Jean intently. They were stunned by the sudden calmness and tranquility of her tone. Matt put down the receiver, and Jean stared at Sarah, her mouth open.

". . . And when you fired Margaret for getting into the liquor . . . who do you think it was who really drank it?"

She fixed her glance on her mother and stepfather in turn and continued: "Mom, listen to me. I've been drinking for nearly two years now. Almost every day. I've snuck booze from the house. And stolen it from liquor stores. I've taken money from your purse. I guess I would've drunk rubbing alcohol if I couldn't get anything else."

She sat on the couch quietly. All the drunkeness

had left her, and she faced them cold sober, naked, exposed.

"You're lying." Jean wouldn't believe her.

Sarah shook her head gravely and bowed it.

"Why?" her mother asked, shattered.

"I don't know . . . I don't know," Sarah said. "I don't know."

As Jean, transfixed and motionless, absorbed the cold, hard truth, Matt walked up to Sarah, took her in his arms gently, and carried her to her room.

Chapter Ten

Dr. Marvin Kittredge, psychiatrist, specialist in adolescent problems, especially alcoholism, was giving a lecture at the PTA meeting of Sarah's high school. At the urging of Mrs. Farrell, Jean went. It was more out of guilt than a real concern for Sarah. Matt had urged her to go too, feeling that they should deal with the matter personally, rather than bringing in outsiders. They were ashamed and humiliated by their daughter's behavior and wanted to keep it private.

The auditorium was surprisingly well-filled when Jean got there about fifteen minutes late. She wore a scarf around her head and dark glasses, in a ridiculous attempt to be there incognito.

Dr. Kittredge was a distinguished-looking gentleman of middle age, with a craggy face and silver-gray, stylishly long hair. Dressed in a dark blue, pin-striped suit, he wore silver-rimmed glasses and smoked a pipe, which he now held unlit in his teeth. His presence on the podium was impressive, even though he was of relatively slight stature.

Jean found a seat in the rear of the auditorium, away from the crowd. She wanted to be able to leave as inconspicuously as she had come in.

The president of the PTA introduced Dr. Kittredge to the parents and teachers gathered there. Jean took solace from the fact that she was not alone. She could see the faces of Mrs. Peterson and a few of her neighbors among the audience.

Dr. Kittredge approached the podium to a scattering of applause. He cleared his throat and began in a serious tone: "There are approximately a half-million pre-teen and teenage alcoholics in this country today. And the number is growing."

A hush ran through the audience. A few people turned to their neighbors in disbelief.

He continued: "That's *kids*. All the way down to nine and ten years old." He shook his finger vigorously. "Three out of every four teenagers do some drinking. One out of twenty has a serious drinking problem. One in ten will become an alcoholic. Alcoholic-related arrests of young people have increased seven hundred percent over the past four years. It may take an adult fifteen years to become an alcoholic. It takes a teenager fifteen months."

Jean shuddered at the thought. Sarah an alcoholic? Impossible. But she did say she'd been drinking for almost two years. Jean started to get up; she wanted to leave, but Kittredge's words were hypnotic.

"Most of them never have blackouts . . . or the D.T.'s . . . or psychotic episodes. And you won't find them hunkered down in doorways on skid row."

Sinking down in her seat, Jean felt as if a hundred eyes were on her—accusing, condemning.

"You find them in schools. At football games. On the beach. And with frightening regularity—you find them strewn and broken on our nation's streets and highways." Here he paused and lit his pipe. He puffed on it a couple of times and went on: "Sometimes you find them in the one place you really don't want to look."

He perused the audience. They stared back at him with the eyes of children.

"In your own home!"

Gathering her coat and purse, Jean slipped out of the auditorium. She was feeling weak and nauseated, as if she had been suffocating. She had to get away from the cool, calm, convincing voice of reason.

"You don't have much faith in shrinks, do you, Mrs. Hodges?" Dr. Kittredge asked casually.

"Well, I . . ."

Jean sat in front of his desk. Her face was drawn from many sleepless nights, and she seemed subdued and distracted. Sarah slumped beside her, an unwilling participant in the discussion. After Jean had heard Dr. Kittredge's talk, she had gone home distressed. When Matt came home that night, she took a positive and forceful stand for getting Sarah some professional help. She called Mrs. Farrell, who referred her to Dr. Kittredge, and they made an appointment for the following day.

"That's all right," he said, smiling. "Some days I have doubts of my own. Why did you come?"

Jean straightened up in the chair and looked at him directly. "The vice-principal at school thought there might be something . . . wrong with Sarah, and then I heard your speech at the PTA meeting. You seemed to know . . . about that kind of problem. I'm ready to admit that now—that Sarah has some kind . . . of . . . behavior problem."

Dr. Kittredge's voice was stern. "Yes, I spoke with Mrs. Farrell about this. Your daughter tells you she's been drinking almost every day for two years and you call it a behavior problem?"

Bristling at his direct manner, Jean answered angrily. "She wasn't picked up out of some skid row bar, you know. She's only fifteen. You want to tell me she's an alcoholic, or something?"

"That's not my judgment to make," Kittredge replied evenly.

At that, Sarah looked up at him quickly, but then lowered her eyes. Kittredge felt he had made his first contact with her.

"Seems to me," he continued, "a fifteen-year-old who drinks every day has to have a lot to say that nobody's listening to. Somebody better start listening."

"Believe me, Doctor," Jean said earnestly, "I've listened."

"But have you heard?" Dr. Kittredge continued in his temperate, professional voice. "Kids develop drinking problems like anybody else, because they're troubled or lonely or frightened. Booze helps them to live . . . to face social situations . . . to get through the day . . . Am I right, Sarah?" He examined her thoughtfully, but she turned her head away, sinking deeper and deeper into the chair.

"And it works. For a while. And then it stops working. Because alcohol is a mean and sneaky drug. First it giveth and then it taketh away." Soothingly, but with emphasis, Kittredge directed his words to Sarah. "And one day you know . . . it's going to kill you. Slower than a bullet, maybe. But a lot faster than old age. And you end up just as dead."

Sarah heard his words but would not respond to them. She kept her arms folded across her chest and her head bowed. Jean, a concerned expression on her face, looked at her daughter and then at Kittredge.

"What can we do?" she asked softly.

Kittredge pushed back from his desk and contemplated Jean for a moment. "We could get Sarah's father down here. The four of us could work on this thing."

At the mention of her father, Sarah perked up. She

watched her mother closely, observing her reaction.

"I wouldn't count on getting him here."

"Try," Kittredge told her. "It's important. But there's something important that Sarah has to do . . . on her own."

"She'll do it," Jean said flatly.

But Kittredge ignored her remark and turned to Sarah. "If we're going to accomplish anything, Sarah, you've got to get off the booze. It sets up a wall between us."

"She's not going to be doing any more drinking," Jean cut in. "I'll see to that."

"No, not you, Mrs. Hodges. Sarah."

He spoke softly and slowly to Jean as if she were a child.

"And you?" Jean was upset by his placid demeanor. "Aren't you going to help?"

"Of course I will," he assured her. "But the first step's got to be Sarah's. Alone. Now I'm sure you've both heard about Alcoholics Anonymous." He braced himself for Jean's reply.

"Oh, no," she said defiantly. "That's where I draw the line."

"Then you know about A. A.?"

"Sure." She fiddled with her purse and sat up uncomfortably. "Bunch of old boozers somebody scraped up out of the gutter. She goes there, she'll learn more about drinking than she ever knew before."

"I wouldn't worry about that," Kittredge said, to pacify her. "We're a country of whiskey-heads. Sarah gets permission to drink every time you and your husband hoist that old five o'clock pick-me-up."

Enraged, Jean sat on the edge of her chair, glaring at Kittredge. "You're not going to lay it all on me, Dr. Kittredge. I'm not even sure I did the right thing coming here. I mean, I bring you a child with emotional problems and you try to make her out to be some kind of wino." Jumping up, Jean started to leave, but Kittredge pursued his point.

"And before you'll admit she might have a drinking problem, you'd sooner see her as crazy . . . some kind of a head case. It's not something to be ashamed of."

Jean disregarded his last statement and nudged Sarah on the shoulder. "I think we'd better go."

"And I think it's time Sarah started thinking for herself." He said it harshly, the first time he had altered his tone of voice during the whole discussion. And then, to Sarah, he said gently, "I'd like to talk to you for a few minutes. Alone. How do you feel about that?"

Roused by the intensity of the discussion, Sarah sat up in her chair. She had been only an observer in a matter that would determine her well-being, her life. She paused. Kittredge and Jean waited expectantly for her reply.

"I'll stay."

Jean nodded her head, admitting defeat. "I'll wait outside."

After Jean had left, there was a long silence. Cautiously, so as not to frighten her, Kittredge got up from his desk and came around to sit on the edge, close to Sarah.

"Well?"

"Well, what?"

"Do you think you're an alcoholic?" he asked candidly.

"No. No, I'm not," Sarah replied quickly.

"All right." He got off the desk, walked over to the coffee table where he kept his pipe and tobacco, and filled a briar pipe. He stoked it thoughtfully, his eyes on Sarah the whole time.

"You believe me?" she asked after a span of a few seconds.

"Doesn't make any difference what *I* believe. It's something *you* have to know. About yourself."

"Then I guess I won't be coming back," she declared decisively.

Kittredge raised a gray eyebrow. "Suit yourself."

Getting up from her chair, Sarah started toward the door. She was confused by Kittredge's unassuming, unauthoritative manner. Unsure, she turned back. "If I was a . . ." she started meekly, afraid to say the word. "I mean, I'm not . . . but if I was—how could I tell?"

Kittredge thought a moment before speaking. He wanted to be as exact and descriptive as possible. She was approaching a critical point in their discussion, and he didn't want to frighten her. "You cross a kind of imaginary line. You begin doing things that are destructive to yourself and the people around you. When you recognize that—then you know."

"Well, I don't do that," she said firmly. "And I can stop drinking any time I want."

"Ever get the shakes? Cold sweats? Ever feel like you can't get out of bed and face the day without getting a little booze down you? You know—just an eye-opener."

She withstood the barrage of his words and shook her head, evading his direct look.

"Did you have a drink before you came here today?"

Not knowing whether to admit the truth or to lie, Sarah hesitated, and then, reluctantly, nodded. Kittredge walked back to his desk and scribbled an address on a card. He held it out to her. "Would you like to show me how you can stop drinking? This minute. For good. Never taking another swallow?"

She returned his direct gaze, trying to stop the terrible shaking that was overcoming her. It would be nice, yes, it would be very nice to be rid of that damn shaking forever.

Chapter Eleven

She had been drinking, and the empty wine bottle lay on her bed, the few remaining drops staining the bedspread. Matt and Jean had gone out to dinner with friends, leaving a leftover meatloaf, which she couldn't bring herself to eat. After they left, Sarah had sat in her dark room and listened to the radio, trying to keep her mind off the booze. She pulled the crumpled card from her jeans pocket. She had shown it to Ken that afternoon at school.

"And the creep gave me this card," she had told him, explaining her visit to Dr. Kittredge's office. "And he wants me to go off to some cruddy old A.A. meeting."

"If you want to know, I don't think it's such a bad idea."

"Oh, boy. I'm just surrounded by traitors." She had stood there pouting.

Ken tried to reason with her. "If you're not an alcoholic, what're you afraid to go to the meeting for?"

"Why should I go? Just to please him?"

"How about to please me?" he said as he turned and walked away, a disgusted look on his face.

Furious with Ken, Sarah crumpled the card and threw it on the ground. Then, self-consciously, she glanced around her and picked it up quickly, stuffing it into her pocket.

Now, as she sat drunk and alone, she took the card out and considered attending the meeting. It was being held in the recreation room of a church in the neighborhood, not far from her house. If she rode her bicycle, she could get there in twenty minutes.

She went into the bathroom, threw some cold water on her face, and brushed her hair. Examining her reflection in the mirror, she thought, "I don't look like one." Her eyes were only slightly droopy, but her face was full of color and she seemed healthy. In Kittredge's office, the idea of giving up drinking had appealed to her. She thought that if she set her mind to it, she could stop anytime. Determined to stay dry tonight, it would be a test of her will power, to prove to Ken, but most of all herself, that she wasn't an alcoholic.

Alcoholic. The word sounded strange. It was different from a drug addict. She always knew that she could never become a drug addict. The thought of sticking a needle in her arm was repulsive. But was she hooked on *booze?* And was it just as hard to get un-hooked? She didn't want to believe it. She wasn't an alcoholic. She wasn't like those bums downtown sprawling on the sidewalks and huddled in the doorways. She just liked to take a little drink now and then to calm her nerves. That was all.

She debated whether or not to go down to the A. A. meeting. If she did, was that a sign that she was, indeed, an alcoholic? What if she went down *just* to observe, to see what they looked like so that she could decide if she were one or not. She didn't have to stay or even say her name. She would remain in the shadows; no one would ever know.

Still a little high from the wine, Sarah went into the shed and got out her bicycle. She climbed on it shakily and started out for the meeting place. It was almost nine, and the card said that the meeting started at

eight. She'd be a little late, but that was even better—
she could slip by unnoticed.

As she approached the church, she could see that it
was all lit up inside. She heard the murmur of voices
and the scraping of chairs. Sarah paused, a little unsteadily, at the door. There was a lot of movement
inside, as if they had taken a break.

"What the hell," she thought. "I rode all the way
here; I may as well see what the big deal is. At least
then I can tell Ken that I went."

She entered the room and was taken aback by the
scene. It looked like the junior prom. Most of the
people there were kids her age; but there were people
of all ages, laughing and chatting as if it were a party.
The only difference was that there were no glasses in
their hands.

A small, slight boy with a pleasant smile approached
Sarah. She couldn't judge his age. Although his body
was small, his face seemed old beyond his years. "Hi.
I'm Bobby." His high-pitched voice gave him away.

"Am I in the right place?"

"If you're looking for the A.A. meeting, you are."

"I thought it was a school dance, or something."

"That's close," he said flippantly. "You got a name?"

Sarah was surprised at the boy's obvious ease and
maturity. He seemed perfectly at home at this meeting
for alcoholics, as if he had been here many times before.

"My name's Sarah."

"Well come on, Sarah, I'll put you in touch with a
doughnut."

They walked across the room to a chorus of friendly
hello's and how-are-you's. Sarah couldn't believe that
all those happy people had a problem. They walked to
the refreshment center, where a girl with long, black
hair and a cheerful face, was serving.

"You can't tell me that all these kids . . ."

"That's right," Bobby said. "Everyone of them. Carol, this is Sarah. Would you see that she gets properly nourished? I've got to get my head together for the ordeal."

Sarah watched in disbelief as Bobby went off. "Wow, he sure is a smart little kid."

"He sure is," said Carol. "He'll be starting high school next year, and he's only eleven." She pointed to the refreshments. "Coffee or punch?"

"Punch."

"Your first meeting?" Carol asked as she poured the punch into a paper cup.

"Uh huh. And my last."

Carol handed Sarah the cup and answered thoughtfully, "I remember the first day I came through those doors. I said to myself: 'This place is a leper colony and I'm no leper.'"

Sarah was startled by her frankness.

Carol's face became serious, and she went on.

"I killed an old man while I was drunk. Ran him over like rags in the street. Not much of an old man, I'll admit. But his grandchildren sure miss him. And I've got his face scratched into my brain for the rest of my life."

She pushed away the painful memory and forced a smile. Sarah seemed a little upset at her admission.

"Hey, listen . . . you're not an alcoholic. You don't have to worry about anything like that. Coffee break's almost over. This next part of the meeting is kind of fun. Go find yourself a seat."

The group resettled itself in the rows of folding chairs, which faced a minister's pulpit used for the rostrum. The room was a bit cluttered and dusty. It seemed to have been used for many gatherings and purposes.

Bobby, seated in the first row, motioned for Sarah

to join him. She hesitated, feeling ambivalent, but the boy's gestures were so determined that she couldn't refuse. She moved in next to him.

"You're really not one of them—a little kid like you," she said.

Bobby grinned and didn't answer. He pointed to the rostrum where the leader was calling the meeting to order.

"We have a birthday tonight. Celebrating one year of new life and sobriety—Bobby R."

Sarah watched as the small boy stood up beside her to the overwhelming applause of the audience. He stepped into the aisle as the members began to sing "Happy Birthday to You." Sarah noticed a woman carrying a birthday cake with one candle. She came from the back of the room and brought it up to Bobby, who took a deep breath, and with mock strength, blew the candle out, to the thunderous applause and laughter of the audience.

Bobby stepped to the rostrum, his head barely visible over the edge. The leader offered him a chair to stand on. Suddenly, the room was quiet. All eyes were on Bobby.

"Hi. My name's Bobby R., and . . . I'm an alcoholic."

Sarah sat up and watched him closely. What dumb ritual were they making him perform?

"Hi, Bobby!" the members said cheerfully.

"I want to thank you all for that cake. I couldn't have gotten it without your help, and your patience, and your understanding."

Surprised by his frankness, Sarah looked around her to gauge the reactions of the others. They were all laughing and looking up at Bobby with affection and friendliness. A few nodded their heads in agreement.

"I want to thank you for the hardest year of my life. And the best. I want to thank you for my life."

It seemed to Sarah that the audience generated a kind of warmth. And the people actually seemed to be enjoying themselves.

"I may only be eleven," Bobby said, "but my liver thinks it's sixty. People never wanted to believe that I was a kid."

The members laughed, but Sarah didn't think it was so humorous. She could sense a deeply serious note in the boy's voice.

His face became grave, and she could see why her first impression had been that he was older than his actual years.

"See, I started drinking about the time I started to walk. My brothers would get me to sipping pop wine just for the fun of watching the little kid get sloshed. By the time I was nine I was taking milk laced with Scotch to school in my thermos. And I wasn't the only kid doing that either. Some days half the class was smashed. And the school never even knew it. They were too busy sniffing around the bathroom for pot smoke."

He paused dramatically, letting the words sink in. Sarah sat up with deep interest.

"You know what I found the hardest part about being a drunk? The lying." A murmur went through the crowd. Sarah winced.

"You've got to be all the time lying to your folks, and lying to your friends, and to yourself."

Her attention focused on Bobby's face, Sarah was mesmerized by the sound of his words. They struck a familiar chord.

"You'd think they wouldn't have cared—my folks. After all, they thought it was pretty funny when I was going around begging sips of beer. Or when I snitched Uncle Mike's cocktail glass and went off and hid in the closet with it. But when I came to them and said, 'Hey, Mom, hey Dad . . . guess what: I'm an alcoholic'

—they didn't think that was so amusing. See,"—he looked directly at Sarah who gave him an encouraging smile—"they'd rather I'd have been anything else—a cat burglar, a Communist . . . not that I blame them. I didn't want to admit it myself. And anyway, it wasn't their problem. Not anymore."

He paused, his adult composure slipping away as he relived the terrible moments: "It was mine. And I had to kick and crawl and puke myself to the place where I could admit it. I had to lose enough friends, and be doing lousy in school, and get so damn disgusted with myself . . ."

His slight body started to tremble noticeably. He stopped and took a sip of water.

"And hate myself so bad that I could finally look in the mirror and say: face it, you're an . . ."

His eyes searched for Sarah, but her seat was empty. He could just catch sight of her back as she headed for the door. But something made her turn—Bobby's pause—and she faced him.

". . . an alcoholic. And if you don't get some help, you're going to die."

Sarah's hand was on the doorknob, just about to turn it, when Carol stepped up behind her.

"Sarah?"

She spun around.

"I hope to see you again," Carol said softly.

Without answering, Sarah pulled the door open and ran to her bicycle. She jumped on it and pedaled furiously until she reached her house, trying to forget the meeting. But Bobby's tender yet experienced face and his painfully honest words had left their mark.

Chapter Twelve

The window shades in Dr. Kittredge's office were drawn, but the afternoon light seeped in around the edges. The gentle hum of the air conditioner played in the background. A moment of uncomfortable silence prevailed, while the participants returned to their corners to prepare for the next round.

Dr. Kittredge, smoking his pipe thoughtfully, sat in a black leather armchair. Sarah and her mother were seated on the couch. Jerry Travis, just in from San Francisco, was hunched in another armchair identical to Kittredge's.

They sat in a tight group, so close that their knees almost touched. Jerry, his jacket hung on the back of his chair, his shirt collar open, and his tie off, seemed the most ill at ease. Jean was resigned, her face grim. And Sarah, her face hard and set in a frown, looked down at her clenched fists.

Reclining in his armchair, Kittredge was a silent observer. Patiently, he waited for the first speaker.

"Come on, Jerry," Jean began. "You slip fifty bucks into her purse, and you're off to San Francisco. But you leave the problems behind. With me."

Jerry looked awkwardly at Kittredge, who remained aloof. Straightening up, he assumed an easygoing attitude.

"I see the terrific job you've done with them."

"I suppose you could have done better."

"I think I could. I haven't forgotten the way you turned Nancy against her father."

He looked to Kittredge for support, but the doctor only puffed on his pipe contemplatively. Jerry turned to Sarah, but she kept her head down, too ashamed to watch the hostility between her parents.

"Nancy didn't need any help," Jean said, her expression weary, as if she had explained this to him many times before. "She was old enough to remember how it was when you were around."

"And what about my Sarah? I leave my baby with you and what's-his-name. You make her so damned unhappy she starts in boozing before she's old enough to give up paper dolls."

Stung by his last remark, Jean countered, "Oh no you don't—you're not going to blame me for that, Jerry. I'm not the one who filled her head with all those beer-bottle dreams about painting in the Oregon woods."

Jerry ran his hand through his dark, thick hair, his eyes flashing wildly. "What would you know about any kind of dreams? The only dream you ever had was how to lock some poor slob into a nine-hour slot so you could sit around until noon in your housecoat."

"How would you know what I did until noon? You were never around enough to . . ."

Kittredge shifted his position and brought his chair forward abruptly. Jerry and Jean were startled into silence by his sudden movement.

"Hey, Sarah," he said in a deep, calm voice, in stark contrast to the high-pitched screaming of the others. "You got anything to say about all this?"

She looked from one parent to another. They stared back at her pathetically, as if waiting for a reward for their performance. Unclenching her fists, she clasped her hands and started to speak, but the words were caught in her throat.

"You've got a voice here," Kittredge went on. "An equal voice. That's what family therapy is all about."

Sarah looked at him searchingly but was still reluctant to answer.

"Okay, let's try it this way. What would you say to your folks if you could get them to listen to you for once? Really listen . . . ?"

She stared at him mutely. He could sense her desire to speak and realized her inability to start.

Kittredge turned to Jean and began for Sarah: "Mom . . . what I really wish is . . ." He nodded his head to Sarah telling her to take over. She began with difficulty.

"Mom . . . what I really wish is that you and Dad didn't fight all the time. I wish you loved each other. I wish we were all together again."

"Honey," Jean said, "you know that's impossible."

Her voice found, Sarah continued with momentum. "Then I wish you loved me the way I am . . . and that you didn't always expect me to be Nancy or somebody I'm not." She was stunned, herself, by the painful admission.

Jean and Jerry both hung their heads, suffering along with their daughter. Jean wiped her eyes with a tissue.

"And Dad . . ." Kittredge started for her.

"Daddy," Sarah whispered, the tears, which she had held back for so long, falling. "Daddy, I love you. And I want to come live with you. *Now.*"

Fidgeting in his chair, Jerry was aware of all the eyes that were on him. The salesman in him came out, and he put on an ingratiating smile.

"Come on, puss—you know your mom won't go along with that."

"Yes I will."

"You will?"

"I'll let her go with you," Jean said sadly, turning to Kittredge. "Obviously I haven't been doing a very good job with Sarah. I thought I was . . . I tried."

"Don't tell me—tell her."

"I do love you, Sarah." She twisted the tissue in her hands, looking at her daughter mournfully. "I love you the best way I know how. But maybe some kind of change would be best. So . . . you have my permission to go live with your father."

Sarah's heart beat quickly in anticipation of her father's reply, but part of her sympathized with Jean.

The air conditioner droned in the background, and finally Kittredge spoke for Sarah.

"Dad . . . ?"

Jerry cleared his throat nervously. His eyes darted from his daughter to Kittredge. "You know, honey, how much I want to have you with me . . ."

No, she thought, he can't be saying that. My daddy wouldn't let me down, not now, not when I need him the most . . .

Jerry continued, his voice cracking. "But I'm away on the road so much of the time. I live out of a suitcase. What kind of a life would that be for you . . . ? I mean, don't you really think a girl is better off with her mother?"

All three faces stared back coldly.

"Damn, I can hardly look out for myself, let alone a fifteen-year-old kid." He smiled meekly at Sarah. "You understand, don't you, puss . . . ?"

Even Kittredge's profesional demeanor was shaken by Jerry's cowardly words. They all stared at him, more out of pity than anger.

"Hey, what is this? What's everybody looking at me for? It wasn't my idea to come here, you know. You needed someone to hang all the blame on, right? Make me look bad in front of my kid. Well, I don't have to sit around here and take that!"

Panicking, he grabbed his jacket from the back of the chair and started for the door.

"Nobody's going to put it all on me."

Too devastated to speak, Sarah stared blankly at the slammed door. Her eyes were dry, her hands steady, but her body was numbed and her spirit crushed. Silently, Jean moved toward her daughter, putting her arms around her. But Sarah pushed them away. Zombie-like, she stood up and without a word left the office.

Jean followed her, head down as if in prayer.

"Sarah, honey . . ." Jean said tentatively. "We could . . ." But she was struck by her daughter's glazed look and decided to drive home in silence.

Once at home, Sarah went up to her room. She hadn't spoken to Jean during the entire ride.

Tearfully, Jean walked into the kitchen to make herself a cup of coffee. After the coffee was made, she had a cup and thought she would go up to Sarah's room to see if Sarah was hungry. She knocked on the door. There was no answer. Hesitantly, she opened it. The room was empty. Pieces of Sarah's piggy bank were scattered all over the floor.

Jean ran to the shed. The red bicycle was missing. Frantic, she ran inside to call Matt.

Chapter Thirteen

"Those phone calls, all those damn unanswered phone calls," Sarah thought as she rode toward the beach. What if he *had* been there, it wouldn't have done her any good. He probably didn't answer the phone on purpose—the bastard. All those dreadful nights when she had been in tears, hanging on to the vague hope that her father would be there to save her. All those times he had promised to come see her, to take her to Oregon. "Artist—he's a liar and a cowardly one at that!" she thought as she rode hard, passing the stables where Ken kept his horse and turning onto the beach where the party had been held.

It was late afternoon, and the beach was deserted. Sarah walked her bike to a secluded spot and sank down in the sand. Picking up a handful of sand, she let the grains run through her fingers as she stared out at the blue-green ocean. Remembering the day she and her father had talked about their dreams and how happy she had been then, brought tears to her eyes. He seemed to be the answer to all her problems. But, now, her dreams were shattered, and she had to rethink her plans.

What if I drowned myself? she thought morbidly. Who would really care? It would be better; then they wouldn't have to worry about her and where she was going to live. Her problems would be over, and so would theirs. But she would never see Ken again, never ride Daisy, never play with Laurie, or have children of her own. She didn't want to drown—she wanted to live. But *they* wouldn't let her!

Burying her head in her hands, Sarah began to cry. Her body shook convulsively with her sobs, but there was no one around to hear them. Exhausted, she lay down on the sand, which was still warm from the sun. Eyes closed, she listened for awhile to the rhythmic pounding of the waves and then slept.

When she awoke, it was dark. For a moment she was confused, but the soothing sound of the waves brought her back to reality. Her throat felt dry and a familiar ache filled her body. She got up, her body leaving an imprint in the sand. She must have slept for hours, and now she was cold and damp. She pushed her bicycle toward the road and mounted it, heading for town. She didn't have to think about where she was going; it was instinctive.

Propping her bike up alongside the window, Sarah pressed her nose against the glass and stared hungrily at the bottle—a child in a candy store.

A well-worn station wagon drove up to the liquor store. A middle-aged, black-haired man walked toward the entrance.

"Hey, mister . . ." Sarah held out a ten-dollar bill. Her face was tense, her eyes big. "It's my father's birthday tonight, and my mom sent me down here to pick up some vodka for the punch. And I wonder could you go in there and . . . buy it for me?"

He looked down at her in disgust, pulling away as she shoved the money toward him. "I'm not buying liquor for any kids. You tell your mother to call and have them deliver it."

A woman who had been standing nearby started to enter the store. As soon as Sarah moved toward her, she shook her head and pushed past Sarah into the store.

Next Sarah spotted a young couple. They only smiled at each other and shook their heads when she asked.

Desperate, she wandered into the store as nonchalantly as possible. The store owner watched her from the corner of his eye. Just as she put her hand around a pint of vodka, he stepped behind her and grabbed it.

"What the hell do you thing you're doing, girlie? I could have you arrested for that. Just get out of my sight!" He shoved her roughly out the door.

Trembling, Sarah walked to the corner of the street and stood under a lamp. Her face was pale, and she broke into a cold sweat. Under the street light, she looked like a lost kitten searching forlornly for its mother.

A beat-up Volkswagen bus, full of young men, pulled up, and a grim determination gripped her. What did she have to lose? Rejected by her father, scorned by Ken, pitied by her mother, Sarah had lost all perspective. Nothing mattered to her any more. Nothing except getting that alcohol down her throat. Instead of drowning herself in the ocean, she would drown in booze.

Standing by the curb, she watched the four young men, who looked like they were in college and barely old enough to drink themselves. They seemed rowdy and playful, out for a night on the town.

The driver, slim, with brown hair, got out of the van.

Sarah blocked his path, her outstretched hand shoving the ten-dollar bill in his face. "Would you guys buy met a fifth of vodka? I'll give you the money."

"I don't think so," he said, as he pushed his way past her.

"I'll do anything you want." She was surprised by her own voice. It sounded different, as if it belonged to another. She was somewhere else, observing—not part of this body.

The driver looked at her curiously. She bent into the window and repeated the offer to the others. "I'll do anything you want," she said, looking into the surprised faces of the three other boys.

They poked each other shyly, and then, as a group, nodded eagerly.

"Get in," a heavyset boy with curly hair told her. She handed the driver the money and got into the back seat. Climbing over the heavyset boy, she sat in the middle. She felt strange; scared and awkward. But something deeper and more persistent was driving her to do what she was doing. She had no control; she was merely acting out the impulses of her body.

The boys joked and made sly comments to each other about her presence, working up their courage.

"Hey, what's your name?" the heavyset boy asked her.

"Sarah."

"Sarah what?"

"Just Sarah."

"Well, just Sarah, my name's John, this here is Pete, the one in the front is Joe, and the driver's Dennis."

They continued to make jokes and sly winks behind her back. Finally, Dennis came back with the bag. Sarah reached out into the front seat for her share, but he ignored her and turned on the motor. They rode in silence to the beach. Sarah could hear the heavy breathing of the boys and feel their anticipation. All she could think of, though, was the bottle.

They got out of the van. Sarah looked at Dennis impatiently but was afraid to speak up first. He pulled out a bottle from the bag and put the other bottle on the front seat of the van, shutting the door.

Wretchedly, Sarah watched as the boys formed a semicircle around her, taunting her with the bottle and leering at her.

Pete held the bottle up to his lips, gave a war whoop, and took a large swallow. He passed it to Joe, who did the same, passing it to John, and then Dennis. They seemed to be enjoying their sadistic game of monkey-in-the-middle.

Sarah was close to tears, her face strained and her eyes frightened. They were treating her as if she were an animal—worse—and she was taking it. Why was she letting them play this degrading game with her? Just to get at her precious booze. If her mother could see her now, or her father. What would they think? Would they think that she was sick, had to be put away? All these thoughts went through her mind as she reached out for the bottle.

"Hey, what about me? I paid too, you know."

"Right, you did," John said. "Here you go, babe." He tossed the bottle to her, but it sailed past her head, into the hands of Dennis, who held it teasingly above him.

"Hey, come on fellas . . ." she pleaded. She moved toward Dennis, her hands outstretched. Joe came running up from behind and tripped her. She landed on her knees. Crawling, she grabbed for the vodka.

"Baby want her bottle," they taunted her.

"We better let her have it," Dennis said.

"Finally," she thought, as she got up and walked over to accept it.

But, with a diabolical smile on his face, he threw it over her head again, and the malicious game was repeated.

They kept it up until the bottle was almost empty, and Sarah was a frantic, trembling heap. She sank down on the hard-packed sand, exhausted, whimpering like a wounded animal.

"You promised. You promised."

"You made some promises too," John reminded her.

"Okay . . . please . . . just gimme the bottle."

"All right, friends. Step right up," he said. "The name of the game is Spin the Bottle. Winner gets first go-round."

The four boys kneeled around Sarah in the hard-packed sand. She watched, dazed and wide-eyed, as John spun the bottle, its contents spilling out onto the sand and seeping into the ground. The bottle stopped spinning, pointing at Dennis.

"And we have a winner!"

"I don't think I . . . want . . . to . . ." Dennis said, suddenly losing his cool.

The other two boys seemed ashamed of their behavior too, as they watched Sarah's pathetic, tear-stained face.

But John didn't give up. He spun the bottle again. It landed pointing away from him but he walked around until he was directly in front of it. "What do you know? I guess I win the kewpie doll."

"Please . . ." Sarah said, hardly conscious of her behavior.

He held the bottle up and looked at it closely. There was just about a half-inch left. With a cruel look in his eyes, he lifted the bottle to his mouth and drained it.

Sarah whimpered, still kneeling on the ground.

"Your bottle's in the bus, love."

She jumped up and ran to the bus with a burst of energy. The boy made an obscene gesture to his friends, who stood in a frightened knot, and followed Sarah.

She climbed into the bus, and he entered the driver's side and handed her the bottle. She clawed at it ferociously, trying to break the seal. He was groping under her shirt and pulling at the buttons.

"Wait a minute, wait a minute," Sarah shouted. She poured the liquid down her throat, pausing only for air and then swallowing again. The boy started the engine and moved to a different part of the parking lot, away from the lights and the eyes of his friends. He turned to Sarah, who was cradling the bottle in her arms protectively.

"No . . . no . . . You can't have it."

"I don't want the damn bottle," he said, reaching over to her. "Just put it down for a second. You promised. Remember?"

She looked at him blankly, and then remembered the deal. "Okay, okay. But don't take the bottle away."

He put the bottle at her feet and moved close to her, the weight of his body making the van squeak. His face came into focus, and she pushed it away. He was breathing hard and fumbling under her shirt with his cold hands. He covered her face with slobbering, wet kisses, and she held her breath. His hand reached for the zipper on her jeans. She tried not to think about what was happening to her, only that the bottle was waiting—a prize—when it was all over. She closed her eyes tightly, a limp doll in his hands.

When it was all over, the boy fell asleep, his heavy bulk almost suffocating Sarah. She managed to pull herself from under his body and got dressed in the cramped front seat. She opened the door and peered out of the van.

The three boys saw the light go on in the bus and came over. The driver pushed his friend over to the other side of the seat in disgust and motioned for Sarah to get in the back. They dropped her off in front of the liquor store, without saying a word.

Catching a glimpse of herself in the darkened window of the store, Sarah was shocked at her appearance. Her hair was matted and full of sand. Her eyes had dark circles under them, and her face was streaked with a mixture of tears and dirt. A button on her shirt was torn off, and her jeans were wrinkled. She stared at herself unemotionally, detesting the image but not connecting it with anyone she knew. She felt removed, anesthetized, and numb. Her bicycle was still in front of the liquor store. She climbed onto it and pedaled slowly, not knowing where to go. She saw the lights of the stable up ahead, and a longing came over her. Maybe Ken would be there; she would go to Ken.

Riding up to the stable, which was quiet except for the shuffling and snorting of the horses, Sarah strained her eyes for Ken. She could see that his car was parked by the entrance to Daisy's stall. She left her bike leaning against the fence, took the bottle out of the basket, and walked toward the stall.

Inside, she found that Daisy's stall was empty and that her tack was missing. Ken must have gone for a ride along the beach.

Settling in a corner of the stable on some old horse blankets, Sarah decided to wait for him to return. She had almost half the vodka left, and she sipped it pensively, but she was clearly sinking deeper and deeper into a drunken stupor. She took an enormous swallow, almost choking herself, and she began to gag. She stood up, gagging and retching, and ran to the edge of the stable. Moaning, her body trembling, she wiped her mouth on her sleeve, but brought the bottle to her lips again.

She heard the sound of a horse's hooves and hid behind a bale of hay. She saw that it was Ken leading Daisy and talking to her affectionately.

"You wait here, Daisy. I want to tell Mom I'll be a little late."

He tied the horse's reins to a post and patted her on the rump as he walked to the phone.

Sarah, clutching the bottle, staggered over to the horse and looked at it. "Why do you think . . . I mean, why do you really think . . ."

Tears welled up in her eyes, and they spilled over the bottle as she raised it for one last swallow before letting it slip to the ground.

Unsteadily, she put one foot in the stirrup, which was much too high for her. With unaccustomed strength, she hoisted herself into the saddle and grabbed the reins. Her mind was blank but filled with inexplicable terror. She shrieked, gave the horse a tremendous kick, and dug her heels into its sides. The horse bolted out of the stable.

Ken came running out of the tack room, horror-stricken. "Sarah! What are you doing?"

The horse took off with Sarah miraculously holding on—flapping like a rag doll. Scared and uncontrollable, the horse, the whites of its eyes gleaming, galloped through the field adjoining the stable. Semiconscious, Sarah pulled the reins first to one side and then to the other, confusing and frightening the animal. It jumped over hedges and ran through low bushes. After a few frantic minutes, it reached the straightaway and settled into a canter.

The lights of the cars on the highway loomed before them. Somewhere in the back of Sarah's bewildered mind, she remembered that Ken had told her something about lights and Daisy, but she didn't know what. Impulsively she guided the horse toward the lights.

All around her, horns were honking. A man in a

uniform was bending over her, shining a flashlight in her eyes.

"What's happening?" she asked, dazed.

"You all right, honey? You've been out for a while."

She looked into the solemn face of the man. He pointed toward a crowd of people. Near them, she could make out the shape of a horse lying on its side. She heard an ear-shattering whine, and then she realized what had happened.

"Daisy . . . Daisy . . ." she cried, getting up. Frozen with fear, she saw the grim face of Ken, watching as the policeman raised the gun.

"Wait," he said, tears streaming down his face. "Is there any chance? Just . . . a chance?" He turned to the veterinarian, who shook his head sadly. The policeman raised his gun again, and taking careful aim, fired.

At the sound of the gunshot, Sarah instantly became cold sober, as if it had brought her back to reality. She walked over to Ken and lightly tapped his shoulder: "I'm sorry I killed your horse . . . Ken . . . Ken, look at me . . . I'm sorry I'm alive . . ."

He looked right through her as if she weren't there and then walked toward the waiting police car.

Sarah started after him, feeling as if he had just stuck a knife through her heart. She staggered toward the outstretched arm of the policeman, and then, suddenly, she darted toward the highway and the oncoming cars.

"Hey . . . hey you, come back here." He ran after her frantically. An oncoming car swerved, its brakes screeching. The policeman clutched her by the back of her shirt and picked her up, cradling the sobbing, quivering creature in his arms.

Chapter Fourteen

After Jean had called Matt at the office, she had dialed Dr. Kittredge's number. His nurse had answered.

"I must talk to the doctor right away," Jean had said. "It's urgent."

"I'm sorry," the nurse replied, "the doctor is in with a patient. Can I take a message?"

"It's an emergency," Jean screamed. "My daughter! She's run away!"

"Just a minute, Mrs. Hodges. I'll see if I can interrupt him."

Dr. Kittredge got on the phone. He told her not to worry, to calm down, and to call the airport to see if Jerry had left yet. "It's a normal reaction to her father's rejection. Don't worry, Mrs. Hodges. Just see if you can get Mr. Travis to go over there so that she can talk to him when she gets home."

Jean had been able to reach the airport in time and had left a message for Jerry. She walked to the window and saw that the taxi was just letting Jerry off in front of the house. She ran to the door.

"I got your message at the airport. Where has she gone?"

"I don't know," Jean said tearfully. "She's just gone. "It's been all day, since we left the doctor's office.

Matt's talking to the police again. Oh Jerry . . . what have we done?"

Matt stepped up behind Jean and put his arms around her. "I'm sorry, Jerry. They don't have anything to report yet."

Standing by the open front door, Jean looked out. It was after ten. Sarah had been missing for over eight hours. Where could she be?

Returning to the living room, she watched Jerry sitting on the couch. He was gazing off into space, puffing furiously on a cigarette, his feet on the table. Suddenly the tension and pressure were too much for her. She lashed out at him. "You know why she did this, don't you?

"Sure I do—because you dragged her to that bloody shrink. You treat a kid like a neurotic, how do you expect her to behave?"

As he watched the two pinched faces locked into their mutual hatred, Matt felt awkward. He went to the den, returning with a bottle of Scotch and three glasses. In the doorway he listened to their accusations.

"She ran away because you rejected her," Jean said, her anger rising.

"I rejected her? You're the one who said you didn't care if she stayed or left."

"And you have about as much sensitivity as . . ."

"Ease up, Jean," Matt said, stepping forward with the peace offering. "C'mon, Jerry. We're all rational adults here. Sarah will be all right. Here, have some of this—it'll help."

He handed a glass of Scotch to Jerry and one to Jean. They both accepted it gratefully, recognizing a momentary truce.

Jerry started to raise the glass to his lips but then stopped. A strange look came over his face. He stared at the amber liquid in the glass and put it down quickly.

"I think I'll pass."

Jean, too, studied the glass in her hand before bringing it to her lips and then set it down next to Jerry's. They both looked at Matt. With an embarrassed shrug, he placed his glass next to theirs.

As he was collecting the glasses and the bottle, the phone rang. They all stood still for a long, painful moment while the piercing shrill sound of the phone filled the room.

"I'll get it," Matt said, as he walked toward the phone.

"Hello, yes . . . Just a minute, I'll put her mother on the phone."

He handed the phone to Jean. She listened intently, her face drawn. She closed her eyes in relief and then replaced the receiver.

"They've found her. Drunk. Out on the highway. They've taken her to Valley Hospital."

"Now . . . now are you gonna lock me up?" Sarah was gasping for air. She had just heaved the metal water pitcher into the hospital window, sending the shattered pieces all over the floor. Kittredge, biting on the stem of his pipe, was sitting next to her bed, calmly observing.

Enraged at his unwillingness to react, Sarah got off her bed and pulled the mattress off, stomping on it.

"You're not crazy, Sarah."

"What am I then? I'm not like other people, Dr. Kittredge." She dragged the mattress back onto the bed and sat on it. "Nothing I do works out. I hurt the people I love. I destroy everything I touch . . ." She looked into his eyes, pleading for the answer.

"You crossed that imaginary line. You're beginning to recognize it."

A look of remembered horror crossed her face, and she started to cry.

"I killed Ken's horse."

"That's right. You did."

"He'll never forgive me."

"He may not."

"I picked up a guy for booze." She recalled the moment with disgust.

"That's something you've got to forgive yourself for."

"I don't feel good. Why . . . why was I put on this earth if I have to feel so rotten all the time? Do something! Help me!"

He looked at the slight girl, dressed in the anonymous white hospital gown. How many times had what almost seemed the same pair of beseeching eyes looked up at him? He wished he were a magician and could cure them with the wave of a wand. Now, Sarah was entering the most critical part of her therapy, and he had to tread softly. She had been in the hospital for two days, and he was sending her home today.

"I can't help you, Sarah. You've got to help yourself."

"What kind of a doctor are you?"

"You've got the choice. You can sink to the bottom of a bottle and drown. Or you can climb out. I can't make the choice for you. I can't badger you or frighten you or coax you into it. No amount of therapy or love or gin and tonic is going to make it for you. You've got to make it alone."

"I can't make it alone," she said in a small voice.

"You've got to take the first step. After that there'll be people to help you. I'll help you."

She got off the bed and walked to the window. She gazed out thoughtfully. Abruptly she turned to face him.

"You won't!"

"You know the words, Sarah," he said in his sooth-ing, deep voice. "I can't say them for you. And I can't believe them for you."

Angry and hurt, she spat out other bitter words—"You're no doctor. You're mean and you're ugly and you enjoy watching people suffer. Get out of here."

"There are some people waiting outside for you."

"GET OUT OF HERE!" she screamed, her face turning red. She threw herself on the bed, attacking the pillow, sobbing.

Slowly, he got out of his chair and walked toward the door. Sarah sat up, struggling to get herself under control, and glared at him.

Dressed in her street clothes, Sarah waited in her room.

The nurse came in. "Your parents are waiting out-side, Sarah. Are you ready to go home?"

She nodded reluctantly. She walked to the door and opened it, glancing cautiously up and down the corridor.

Jean and Matt were standing down the hall and came closer when she appeared. A bit apart, looking dis-heveled and pained, was Jerry. Kittredge, standing at the desk, was talking with a nurse.

"It's been a nightmare for you," Jean said, stepping forward and putting her arms around her daughter. "But things are going to be different from now on. And the first thing we have to do is just all . . . forget what's happened."

Sarah remembered the old Jean: ignoring her daugh-ter's cries for help; pushing her to make friends; blam-ing her for all their unhappiness. It was indeed a stark contrast to the Jean who softly, lovingly, and tenderly held her daughter in her arms.

Jerry stepped forward. Sarah's heart stopped when

she saw that he had returned to his old charming self again, but she watched him cynically, not believing his words.

"I don't know what came over me at that therapy session, puss," he said, putting his hand on her shoulder. "Just got a little rattled, I guess. But if my little girl really wants to come to San Francisco with me . . . then . . . couple of weeks I'll have this job tied down for sure and we can talk about . . ."

The same old lines, the same lies. When were they going to learn, when were they going to stop trying to put one over on her—but most of all, on themselves?

"Mom . . . Daddy . . . it won't work the old way. Because what I am . . . you see . . ."

The realization, the strength to say the words, had welled up in her as she saw the empty, tired faces of her parents, as she realized that they couldn't help what they were, but she could help what *she* was.

"I'm an alcoholic."

Jean, momentarily stunned, recovered.

"Don't be foolish, Sarah . . ."

"You got some problems," Jerry said, brushing it off lightly. "Okay, we all do. But I'm sure we can talk them out."

He tried to put his arm around her protectively, shielding her from the truth, but she pushed it away.

"You're not listening. I guess you don't want to hear it. I know I didn't." She looked at Kittredge, who gave her a reassuring nod. "But that's the way it is: I'm an alchoholic."

The words came easily now. Kittredge was right. She had said the words—to herself, to her parents—and she could go on, believing that there was hope. With renewed determination, she faced her startled parents.

"I love you both . . . I think you probably love me

the best way that you can. I do want us to talk. With Dr. Kittredge. But not now. Now there are some people I have to see."

Moving down the corridor slowly but with confidence, Sarah headed toward the two figures seated on the waiting room couch. Her face broke into a wide, relieved smile—the first in a long time. Carol and Bobby stood, returning her smile. She took a deep breath, and they fell in beside her.

They walked purposefully, joyfully bounding down the steps of the hospital, as the adults watched from the doorway.

"Listen," Sarah turned to them when they had reached the sidewalk. "There's something I've got to tell you guys. What I could use right now is a drink."

"Don't worry," Carol told her, taking her hand. Bobby took the other one. "We'll see you through."